THE LENDER LIABILITY DESKBOOK

Peter M. Edelstein, B.A., J.D., LL.M.
Professor of Law, Pace University, Pleasantville, New York
Member of Edelstein & Lochner, Counselors at Law, Armonk, New York
Member of New York, Connecticut, and Florida bars

BUSINESS ONE IRWIN
Homewood, Illinois 60430

This publication is designed to provide accurate and authoritative information in regard to the subject matter covered. It is sold with the understanding that neither the author nor the publisher is engaged in rendering legal, accounting, or other professional service. If legal advice or other expert assistance is required, the services of a competent professional person should be sought.

From a Declaration of Principles jointly adopted by a Committee of the American Bar Association and a Committee of Publishers.

Project Editor: Jess Ramirez
Production Manager: Mary Jo Parke
Designer: Heidi J. Baughman
Typeface: 11/13 Times Roman
Printer: Book Press

Library of Congress Cataloging-in-Publication Data

Edelstein, Peter M.
The lender liability deskbook/Peter M. Edelstein.
p. cm.
Includes index.
ISBN 1-55623-818-5
1. Lender liability United States. I. Title.
KF1035.E34 1992
346.73'073 dc20
[347.30673] 92 10607

Printed in the United States of America

1 2 3 4 5 6 7 8 9 0 BP 9 8 7 6 5 4 3 2

Preface

Whether you are a loan officer, loan administrator, loan assistant; whether you are in loan review or loan processing, or on the loan committee; or whether you are an officer or director, it is hard to be involved in lending today. It is tough to find qualified borrowers, and then it is an ordeal to get the loan approved. After the loan is approved it is still far from closed, and many borrowers require constant hand holding to move them along to the closing. Once closed, loan administration is detailed and tedious.

And now, the mechanical parts of the loan process can seem like fun compared to dealing with old legal theories that are currently being imaginatively asserted by unhappy borrowers against their lenders. These theories are collectively known as the *law of lender liability*. Everyone involved in the loan process—especially loan officers, in addition to being salespeople, financial analysts, economists, managers, and psychiatrists—must now be familiar with this area of the law for their institution's (and their) protection. Indeed, the loan officer is the first line of defense. The nature and duration of the loan officer's relationship with the borrower puts the officer in an extremely effective (and vulnerable) position concerning lender liability issues. The loan officer is usually the first to deal with the borrower and usually remains closely involved throughout the transaction, from loan application to closing and beyond.

This *Deskbook* is intended to assist you by illustrating the risks associated with lender liability and by suggesting the means to avoid or minimize those risks. The format and scope of the *Deskbook* were developed as the result of having worked as counsel to lenders and having gained an appreciation of the various pressures placed on their personnel by the institutions and by the borrowers. The *Deskbook* is designed as a practical and nontechnical guidebook for frequent use. I have tried to take a complex and broad subject and make it manageable by the use of clear and concise explanations, examples, and suggestions.

The *Deskbook* can be read through from beginning to end for those interested in becoming generally familiar with the field of lender liability, or it can be used as a reference source when the need arises.

Part I is an introduction to the basics of lender liability and the potential consequences of a lender's wrongful acts. Each of the most common theories of lender liability is addressed by dividing the analysis into parts: Headnote, Definition, Elements, Discussion, Damages, Illustrative Holdings, and Examples.

The *Headnote* offers a brief introductory statement of the theory of liability. *Definition* gives the common definition of the theory of law (sometimes called a cause of action). *Elements* lists the component parts of the definition, each one of which must be proved by a borrower in order to hold the lender liable. An understanding of the elements will help you in applying the theories and recognizing when your, or your institution's, activities are moving toward a danger zone.

Discussion explains how each theory is applied. *Damages* indicates what the courts may allow a successful borrower to recover from its lender. In some instances, the borrower may not have to repay the loan; in others, it may recover damages from the lender to compensate it for the monetary loss caused by the lender. And in still other cases, the borrower may recover additional damages that are intended to punish the lender when its behavior warrants the court setting an example for others.

Illustrative Holdings offers samples of court decisions based on wrongful lender activity. The *Examples* are illustrations in the form of fact patterns and decisions taken from actual cases. The coverage of each theory ends with *Practical Considerations* offering guidance for dealing with lender liability issues related to that theory.

Part II offers suggestions for avoiding or minimizing exposure to potential lender liability. The suggestions are divided into those applicable when dealing with borrowers (the *Practice* suggestions) and those applicable to documentation (the *Documentation* suggestions).

Part III addresses the special lender liability problems associated with discovering and managing environmental matters, and suggestions are offered for consideration by loan personnel and by lender's counsel.

A Glossary is provided for assistance with some of the legal language, and a detailed Index is provided for easy reference.

Throughout the *Deskbook* the term *lender* refers to the lending institution, and the term *loan officer* refers to the person who does the work, no matter what his or her actual title is.

It was my primary objective to create something of basic, immediate, and real utility to loan personnel. The *Deskbook* is not intended to be a treatise of law and, therefore, does not cover the more esoteric or exotic areas of lender liability. Consult with your institution's counsel for information concerning the less common theories of lender liability, the federal statutes (the Sherman Antitrust Act, the Bank Holding Company Act, the Racketeer Influenced and Corrupt Organizations Act [RICO], the Securities Act of 1933, and the Securities Exchange Act of 1934), or the application of the Federal Bankruptcy Act.

However you use the book, I hope it assists you and makes your job a little easier.

Peter M. Edelstein

Acknowledgment

The Herbert V. Prochnow Foundation of the Graduate School of Banking, Madison, Wisconsin, provided a grant to the author. Pace University, Pleasantville, New York, provided clerical and research assistance and the time to write. The author sincerely thanks the Foundation and the University for their support.

Contents in Brief

Contents

THE LENDER LIABILITY DESKBOOK

PART

I

POTENTIAL LENDER LIABILITY

Chapter One

Introduction to Lender Liability

BACKGROUND

In 1968, a California court held a lender liable to the purchasers of defective homes that were constructed by its borrower. From that case, which is generally regarded as the first to deal with what is now known as lender liability, have followed many judgments against lenders, based on many different theories, and many for amounts far in excess of the original amount of the loan.

The growth of lender liability was due to a confluence of factors during this particular time in the history of banking and law. You may remember that banking used to enjoy a position of great respect and relative insulation from the day-to-day quarrels of the marketplace. To become a banker was a noble calling and a secure one. It was not uncommon for bankers to stay at a single institution for their entire careers, enjoying a comfortable lifestyle with attendant stature in the community.

Then things started to change. The direction of the economy became less predictable. Deregulation and unbundling resulted in lenders becoming more transaction oriented in their quest for noninterest income. Borrowers began to treat lending institutions like retail stores where they could pick, compare, and choose products. Loan officers became more mobile, attracted by better (or apparently better) opportunities; strong customer relationships were not developed or, if developed, not preserved. And lenders, viewed as big, impersonal entities, were attractive targets for litigious customers.

Borrowers apparently got smarter and more sophisticated. Not only were loan terms comparison shopped, but accommodations were bargained for during extensive negotiations, either in the form of informal promises from the loan officer or agreements required to be set forth in the loan documents. No longer was the lender viewed as an institution that provided resources to enhance and exploit the borrower's personal or business opportunities, but rather as another party with which to negotiate, along with vendors and landlords, to obtain the best possible terms. Customers came to believe that lenders no longer provided a personalized service; they merely sold a product for which they should suffer "product liability."

The exact reasons for these changed perceptions may be debatable, but the result is not. Now, if the litigious borrower defaults on the indebtedness or even if something goes wrong with the venture, the borrower creates a list of parties who can be blamed. The lending institution is now one of those parties. And, of course, when a customer sues a lender, the typical juror may find it easier to identify with the customer than with the lender.

THEORIES OF LENDER LIABILITY

The term *lender liability* does not describe a particular wrong upon which a lawsuit may be based (for example, an unhappy borrower does not sue for lender liability), but rather it describes a recognized area of law by which a lender may be held liable for its wrongful acts. The term encompasses various theories of law by which the complaining party (usually the borrower) may assert its rights against the lender.

If a customer feels injured by the lender, the customer selects one or more (usually more) of the available theories and alleges wrongful acts by the lender based on those particular theories. The more common theories of law on which lender liability is based are

- Breach of contract.
- Negligence.
- Fraudulent misrepresentation.
- Nonfraudulent misrepresentation.
- Duress.
- Tortious interference.
- Breach of fiduciary duty.
- Breach of the duty of good faith and fair dealing.

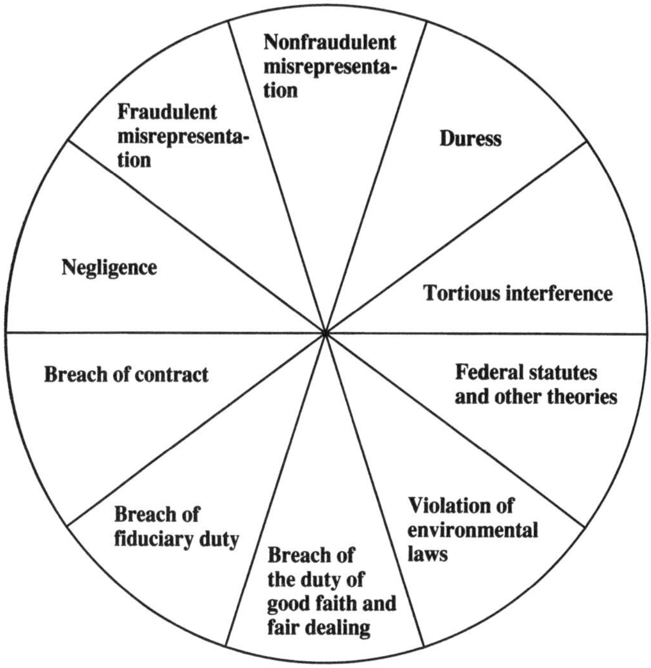

For the customer to recover, the court must be satisfied that all the required elements of the theory or theories selected were proved and that the lender had not raised any valid defenses.

The claim may be asserted initially by the borrower in a lawsuit against the lender or, as is more commonly the case, as a counterclaim asserted by the borrower when the lender sues to collect the debt. The complaining party is called the "plaintiff," and the defending party is called the "defendant."

Potential lender liability can be found in all aspects of and at any point in a transaction—in letters of intent and commitment letters, throughout the loan documents, in the process of loan administration, and even in workout. By being aware of the nature and sources of potential liability, you will be able to avoid or minimize your exposure.

Chapter Two

Breach of Contract

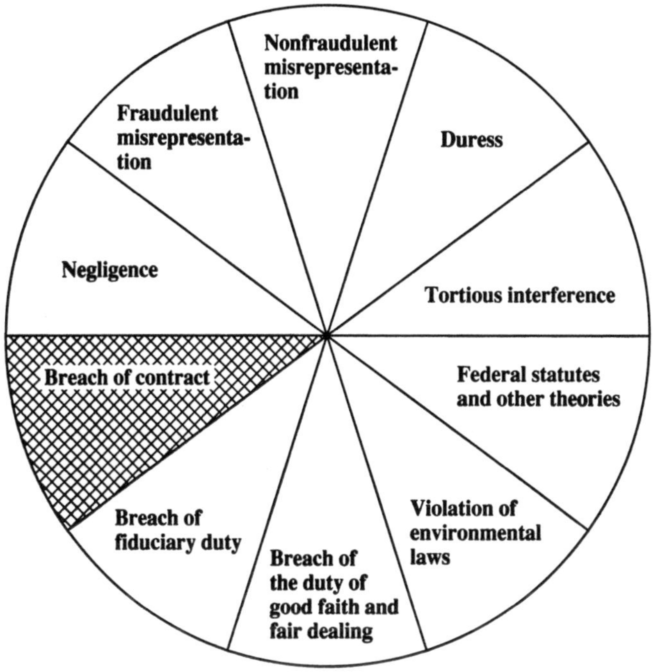

If the law finds that a contract exists and that one party did not comply with its agreements, a remedy will be provided in favor of the other party.

DEFINITION

A *contract* is an agreement that the law will enforce.

ELEMENTS

To recover, the plaintiff must show first that a contract existed, and second, that the defendant breached it. To show the existence of a contract, the plaintiff must generally prove

- Offer.
- Acceptance.
- Consideration.
- Capacity of the parties.
- Legality of purpose.

A breach of contract occurs when a party, without legal excuse, fails to perform in accordance with the terms of his or her agreement.

DISCUSSION

Assume you send, on behalf of your institution, a commitment letter to a proposed borrower requesting its return, signed, with a commitment fee. Your letter may constitute the "offer," which, when signed and returned by the borrower with the fee, may be deemed the "acceptance." The "consideration" consists of the promise or commitment to lend, on the one hand, and the fee paid by the borrower, on the other. If the parties do not suffer any legal disabilities (for example, minority—being under 18 years of age) and the loan is for a legal purpose, a contract is formed. If your institution, without legal excuse, fails to lend in accordance with the terms of the commitment letter, it has breached the contract.

Most contracts made during the course of the banking relationship will be written. However, as a general rule, a written document is not required (even though, in a commercial environment, it is always a good idea to put your agreements in writing). In fact, a contract does not even have to be expressed in words (an "express" contract); it can be implied from the conduct of the parties (an "implied" contract). Contracts can be formal or informal; for example, a structured loan agreement with lots of legalisms is a formal contract, and a simple commitment letter is an informal contract. Regardless of the type, a contract is a legally binding instrument.

Loan officers, naturally, do or say many things intended to result in a contract, with the expectation that their institutions will be legally bound. Problems arise, however, when something done or said casually is later alleged to have been a contract.

The earliest express contract in the lending process is usually the commitment letter. It has enormous legal significance due to its varied purposes: (1) it obligates the lender to lend, (2) it sets forth conditions or events that will relieve the lender from its obligation, and (3) it serves as the plan for the entire transaction to follow. Because each of the terms of the letter may someday be the subject of a legal dispute, the commitment letter warrants great care in its preparation. Whether your institution's view of commitment letters involves the "comprehensive" approach or the "outline" approach, it is imperative to ensure that everything intended to be included in the letter is included, and that everything intended to be excluded is excluded. Once the commitment letter is signed by both parties, it is too late to add to or delete from it, unless the lender and the borrower both agree.

Some of the loan documents themselves are contracts (for example, the loan agreement or security agreement). Generally, any document requiring the signatures of the lender and the borrower may be considered a contract, and both parties will then be bound by its terms. Since a court will look to all relevant documents in the transaction to determine the intent of the parties, beware of inconsistencies in the same or different documents or between what is written and what is said.

A breach of contract may be alleged due to an institution's failure to comply with the promises contained in the loan documents (for example, a promise to lend at a certain interest rate) or failure to comply with promises not contained in the loan documents (for example, a verbal promise by a loan officer to provide financing in the future).

DAMAGES

A successful plaintiff is entitled to recover "compensatory damages." This means the plaintiff will be awarded a sum intended to have the effect of putting it in the same position it would have been in had the defendant performed the contract as required. The damages are limited to those that were reasonably foreseeable at the time the contract was made and that naturally flow from the defendant's breach.

Compensatory damages include the plaintiff's "loss of value," that is, the difference between the value of the promised performance and the value of the actual performance received. For example, if the borrower paid a commitment fee of $500 when the commitment letter was signed and returned and the lender wrongfully failed to make the loan, the borrower has suffered a loss of value to the full extent of the $500.

In addition to the loss of value, the plaintiff may recover "incidental" and "consequential" damages so that the borrower is fully compensated for all of the results of the defendant's wrongful acts. Incidental damages arise directly from the defendant's breach. For example, if the same borrower had to pay another commitment fee to a second lender, that fee would be recoverable as an item of incidental damages. Consequential damages do not flow directly from the act of the defendant but rather from the consequences of the act. For example, if the lender wrongfully failed to lend in accordance with its commitment and that failure caused the borrower to lose a business opportunity, the lender may be liable for the lost profits on the proposed venture, as consequential damages. It is entirely possible that the amount of the plaintiff's lost profits can be far greater than the amount of the loan.

ILLUSTRATIVE HOLDINGS

Lenders have been held liable for

- Failure to lend pursuant to an agreement.
- Failure to lend additional funds pursuant to an oral promise.
- Refusing to fund the remainder of a line of credit.

EXAMPLES

Case A

Facts Bank president told BORROWER that LENDER would lend money to purchase lambs. The parties did not confirm the exact amount of the loan, the date of the loan, the rate of interest, or the terms of payment. Relying on the statement of the bank president, BORROWER signed a contract with Seller to purchase the lambs. LENDER changed its mind and did not lend BORROWER the money. BORROWER sued LENDER for breach of contract.

Decision For BORROWER. The agreement to lend was a contract, which LENDER breached.

Case B

Facts A vice president of LENDER told BORROWER at dinner, "We are going to lend you $10 million for this project." Based on this conversation, BORROWER entered into a contract for the purchase of certain real estate from Seller. LENDER advanced $3 million, which BORROWER paid to Seller as a partial down payment. BORROWER, thereafter, submitted a formal application for the loan, which was rejected. As a result, BORROWER was unable to complete the purchase from Seller and sued LENDER for breach of contract for the loss of the down payment and loss of profit on the project.

Decision For BORROWER for $18.5 million, representing the down payment that was lost and partial loss of profit on the real estate transaction. The promise to lend made at dinner was held to form the basis of a contract, which LENDER breached.

Case C

Facts BORROWER sought and received a firm commitment for a line of credit from LENDER to develop raw land. BORROWER drew down part of the line and then stopped work for the winter. In the spring, after BORROWER's loan officer had been changed, the president of LENDER told BORROWER that LENDER would no longer advance funds from the unused portion of the line of credit. BORROWER could not complete the development and lost the money invested in the project. BORROWER sued LENDER for breach of contract.

Decision For BORROWER. The agreement to provide the line of credit was a contract, which LENDER breached by its failure to fund.

PRACTICAL CONSIDERATIONS

- A promise can constitute the basis for a contract. Do not make or indicate any promises that you may not be able to keep.

- Check for express promises in letters of intent, commitment letters, loan documents, correspondence, and side letters, as well as in conversations.
- Because a contract can be formed from conduct, beware of activities that may be construed as an agreement. For example, repeatedly accepting a late payment, with no comment, may be deemed an agreement to waive the "late charge" or the regular due date of the payment.
- Be familiar with words of "condition," which, when used with a promise, may qualify the promise and avoid the formation of a contract: *if*, *when*, *upon*, *subject to*, *on condition that*, *contingent upon*, *might*, *maybe*, *depending upon*, and *supposing*. For example, in the sentence "We will lend you $1 million *upon* our approval of satisfactory credit reports and appraisals," the promise to lend is conditional. If the condition is not satisfied (approval of satisfactory credit reports and appraisals), no enforceable agreement has been made.

Chapter Three

Negligence

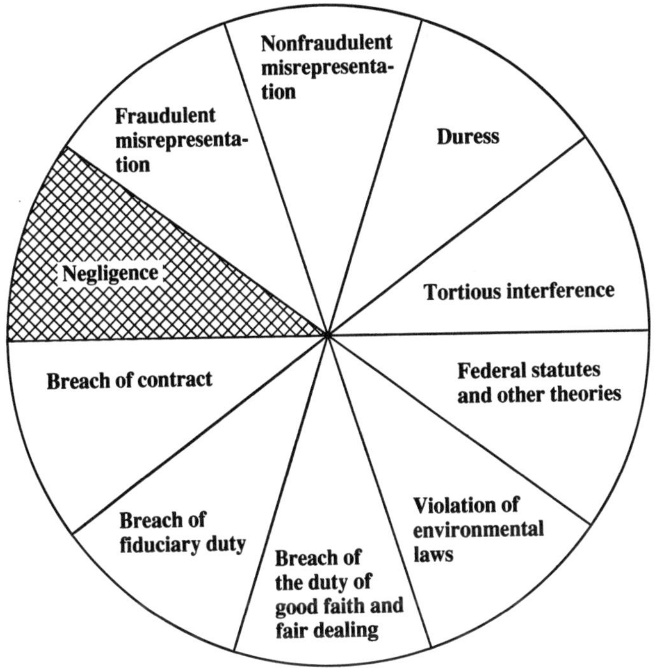

A person failing to act with reasonable care required under the circumstances and causing harm to another will be held liable for the damages caused.

DEFINITION

Negligence is conduct that falls below the standard established by the law for protection against an unreasonable risk of harm.

ELEMENTS

To prove negligence the plaintiff must show

- A duty of care owed by the defendant to the plaintiff.
- A breach of that duty.
- Damage suffered by the plaintiff.
- A causal relationship between the breach of duty and the damage.

DISCUSSION

The theory of negligence deals with careless, rather than intentional, behavior and is frequently associated with automobile cases. If X passed a stop sign and hit your car while you were properly driving through the intersection, X may be liable to you for negligence. The law reasons that X had a duty to stop at the stop sign, X breached that duty, you were injured, and your injury was due to X's breach.

Similarly, courts have found that lenders may have a duty of care to their borrowers and potential borrowers. While this duty is not owed to everyone, nor owed in all circumstances, it may arise from the terms of a contract or by voluntary assumption. For example, if you receive and accept a signed loan application together with an application fee, a contract may exist imposing a duty on your institution to process the application with care. Even if the transaction is not deemed to form a contract, if on receipt of the application you inform the customer that you are processing it, your institution may have voluntarily assumed a duty to do so with care. The mere submission of an application to a lender, without more, probably does not create a duty of care on the part of the lender, but once the duty is found to exist, if the customer is injured due to the breach of that duty, the lender will be held liable.

In determining whether a lender breached the duty of care, the lender's conduct will be compared to the conduct of an imaginary "reasonably prudent lender," in substantially the same circumstances.

DAMAGES

A plaintiff damaged by a negligent defendant is entitled to compensatory damages calculated to compensate the plaintiff for the injuries suffered and to put the plaintiff in the position it would have been in before the negligence. In addition, in appropriate circumstances, the plaintiff may be entitled to "punitive" or "exemplary" damages, which are awarded to punish outrageous conduct and to deter the defendant and others from similar future conduct. The amount of the punitive damages may be substantially more than the amount of the compensatory damages.

ILLUSTRATIVE HOLDINGS

Lenders have been held liable for

- Failure to process a loan application with care.
- Telling a prospective home buyer that the buyer's application for a loan had been approved when, in fact, it had not.
- Failure to prevent construction and sale of seriously defective homes by its borrower (the developer).

EXAMPLES

Case A

Facts LENDER acknowledged, by letter, receipt of a mortgage application and fee from BORROWER and informed BORROWER of the prevailing interest rate and that the approval process would take approximately four weeks. In due course, LENDER mistakenly informed BORROWER that the loan application had been approved for $74,000. Subsequently, LENDER informed BORROWER that it had erred in its original determination and, in fact, BORROWER qualified for no more than a $41,400 loan. BORROWER then applied for and received a mortgage commitment from another bank but, because interest rates had risen, had to pay more for the loan. BORROWER sued LENDER for negligence based on LENDER's failure to exercise due care in processing the mortgage application.

Decision For BORROWER. A contract existed between LENDER and BORROWER, which gave rise to LENDER's duty of care. LENDER carelessly and improperly processed the application in breach of its duty to BORROWER. LENDER's conduct constituted negligence.

Case B

Facts BORROWER applied for a home construction loan. After many telephone calls to LENDER, BORROWER was mistakenly told that the loan was approved. Based on this call, BORROWER started construction of the new home. Approximately two months later, during another telephone conversation, BORROWER learned that the loan had not been approved. BORROWER sued LENDER for negligence.

Decision For BORROWER. Once the bank voluntarily agreed to assist its customer, it assumed a duty and was required to act with due care. Its failure to act with care was a breach of duty and caused injury to the BORROWER. LENDER was negligent.

Case C

Facts LENDER had an arrangement with BORROWER whereby it agreed to finance the purchase of land for BORROWER (who had no significant experience in large-scale construction of tract housing) in return for, among other things, the right to make construction loans for the homes to be built and the right of first refusal to make residential mortgages to the eventual buyers of the homes. Purchasers of defective homes built on the land sued various parties involved in the development, including LENDER, for negligence.

Decision For Purchasers. The court held that LENDER had a duty to the purchasers of the homes to exercise reasonable care to prevent its BORROWER from constructing and selling defective homes. LENDER knew or should have known of the defects in the homes because of its extensive involvement with and control over the venture. The court noted that the bank became much more than a lender content to lend money at interest on the security of real property. It became an active participant in the home construction enterprise and should have foreseen the risk of harm to the purchasers. The success of LENDER's transaction depended entirely on the ability of BORROWER to induce the home buyers to purchase homes in BORROWER's tract and to finance those purchases through LENDER. In addition, LENDER agreed to hold title to raw land for BORROWER on the condition that it be used for residential purposes, and LENDER would further profit by BORROWER exercising repurchase options from LENDER. LENDER knew or should have known that the principals of BORROWER had no experience in a project of the magnitude of the one undertaken, that the venture was thinly capitalized, and that BORROWER could be driven to cutting corners in the construction. All of the elements of negligence were present.

PRACTICAL CONSIDERATIONS

- There will be no liability unless there exists a duty of care. That duty is not owed to everyone. It usually arises in connection with a contract or because the lender voluntarily assumed it.
- Once the duty exists there will be no liability for negligence unless the duty of care was breached; that is, the lender did not act reasonably (did not exercise due care) under the circumstances. Therefore, act carefully.
- Negligence can be found in an act (a "commission") or in a failure to act (an "omission") and at any stage of a loan transaction.
- Ask: How would an imaginary "reasonably prudent lender" act in the circumstances? How does my conduct compare? Should I be doing something I am not doing? Should I stop doing something I am doing?

Chapter Four

Fraudulent Misrepresentation

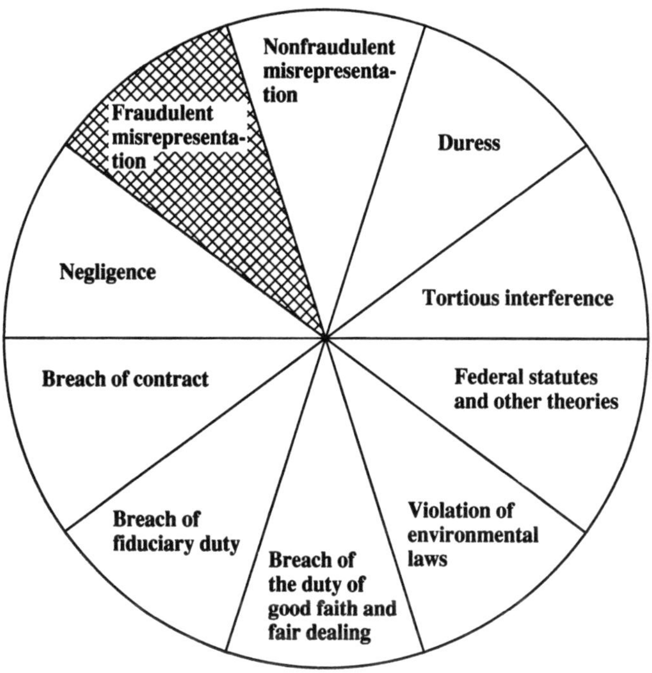

The law will provide a remedy for a person who is harmed by the intentional misrepresentations of another.

DEFINITION

Fraudulent misrepresentation (sometimes called "fraud" or "fraud in the inducement" or "deceit") is the false representation of a material fact, made with knowledge of its falsity and an intent to deceive, that is justifiably relied on by and causes damage to another.

ELEMENTS

To prove fraudulent misrepresentation, the plaintiff must show

- A false representation (a misrepresentation) of a
- Material
- Fact,
- Made with knowledge of its falsity and an intent to deceive, and
- Justifiable reliance by and
- Damage resulting to another.

DISCUSSION

Assume that when purchasing a used car, you relied on the seller's statement that the car had never been in an accident. After the purchase you learned that, in fact, the car had recently been damaged and the seller was the driver at the time. You could claim fraudulent misrepresentation; the representation of fact was false, it was material, it was made by the seller with knowledge of its falsity and an intent to deceive; you justifiably relied on it and were damaged.

If what is represented is true, the theory of fraudulent misrepresentation is not available. The essence of the theory is the falsity; therefore, the plaintiff must show that the representation was false.

The misrepresentation must concern a material aspect of the transaction; that is, would the plaintiff have entered the transaction "but for" the misrepresentation? The test is whether the misrepresentation of fact substantially influenced the decision of the plaintiff to enter the transaction.

A *fact* is a past event, definitely ascertainable and verifiable. It is distinguished from opinions or statements of value, which are generally not facts. Sometimes, however, when a person with superior skill or knowledge (an "expert") gives an opinion or makes a statement of value, it may be considered a fact. For the plaintiff to recover, the plaintiff must have justifiably relied on the misrepresentation. If the plaintiff should have known that the representation was false, or was unaware of the misrepresentation, or would have acted anyway, there will be no recovery for misrepresentation.

The element "knowledge of falsity and intent to deceive," sometimes referred to by its Latin name, *scienter*, can be satisfied by showing that the defendant had actual knowledge of the falsity, or did not believe in the truth of the representation, or had a reckless disregard as to the truthfulness of the representation. A misrepresentation innocently or negligently made does not constitute fraudulent misrepresentation, but it may be the subject of a claim for nonfraudulent misrepresentation, discussed in Chapter 5.

Even if all the other elements are present, the plaintiff cannot succeed unless it can be shown that the plaintiff was damaged. You can intentionally deceive another, but if the other does not suffer damage, there will be no recovery. For example, a seller of land who tells a buyer, intending to deceive the buyer, that the land would be good for farming cannot be successfully sued for fraudulent misrepresentation when the land turns out to be arid and rocky but have a valuable gold deposit beneath it.

DAMAGES

A plaintiff induced by fraudulent misrepresentation to enter an agreement may avoid (rescind) the agreement, receive back any monies paid, and be relieved of any obligations. The plaintiff may recover damages intended as compensation for all the injury caused by the justifiable reliance on the defendant's misrepresentation. Most states have adopted the "benefit of the bargain" rule, which allows the compensatory damages to include loss of profits. Punitive or exemplary damages may also be available when appropriate.

ILLUSTRATIVE HOLDINGS

Lenders have been held liable for

- Representations creating a false impression regarding a decision (or lack of a decision) to declare a default.
- Representations that future financing would be available after an assignment of accounts receivable when, in fact, the lender had already determined not to make the funds available.

- Untrue representations concerning the condition of a borrower that induced another to lend to the borrower.

EXAMPLES

Case A

Facts *State National Bank of El Paso* v. *Farah Manufacturing Company, Inc.*, a 1984 Texas case, in which the plaintiff was awarded over $19 million in damages, is now considered a classic lender liability case. The plaintiff successfully alleged theories of liability for fraudulent misrepresentation, duress, and interference with business relations.

Farah Manufacturing Company (FMC) started in 1919 as a family-owned apparel manufacturer. In 1964, William F. Farah (Farah) became chief executive officer (CEO). In 1967, the company went public and by 1970 had annual sales of $136 million. In 1972, the company suffered a strike and a nationwide boycott. The strike was settled in 1974, but for the 1972–76 period the company showed pretax losses of almost $44 million. In July 1976, the board of directors removed Farah as CEO, and at the annual directors' meeting the following March, he sought to be reinstated as CEO.

In 1977, FMC borrowed $22 million pursuant to a loan agreement that contained a management change clause stating that it would be an event of default if there was a change in executive management that any two lenders considered, for any reason whatsoever, adverse to their interests.

The lenders, of which State National Bank (SNB) was one, in reliance on the management change clause, told the company that if Farah was reinstated, a default would be called. Under the management change provision, the banks had two alternatives in the event they considered Farah's election adverse to their interests: they could declare a default or they could waive the default and accept Farah as CEO. The lenders exercised neither option but, rather, threatened to call a default when, in fact, they were undecided as to what they would do. The threat had its desired effect, and Farah was not elected CEO.

The directors who were finally elected had close ties to the lenders. The new CEO and a member of the FMC board were also members of one lender's board. When the company continued to suffer losses under the lender-approved management, the lenders requested that FMC hire a specific consultant who caused assets to be sold to prepay the company's debt to the lenders.

Farah started a proxy contest, was reinstated as CEO, and turned around the company. The company then brought an action against SNB, basing its claim for fraudulent misrepresentation on the statement that SNB would call the loan if the company reinstated Farah when, actually, the lender was unsure of what action it would take.

FMC introduced evidence consisting of (1) a letter sent by the lenders' attorney to the board of directors stating that the election of Farah was unacceptable to the lenders but that the lenders would consider waiving the default of the management change clause if there was a change in management not involving Farah; (2) a statement by lenders' attorney to the effect that if Farah was elected CEO, the attorney would bankrupt the company and padlock its doors the next day; and (3) a statement by the attorney that the lenders opposed the election of certain board members loyal to Farah.

Decision For FMC, the BORROWER. The court found that the evidence constituted the basis for fraudulent misrepresentation and held

> the lenders had either decided not to declare a default . . . or had reached no decision on the matter. Neither position was conveyed to the board. Regardless of the position taken, the "warnings" (representations) . . . are . . . false threats constituting fraud.

Based on the same wrongful actions by the lenders, the court also found them liable for duress and interference with business relations.

Case B

Facts BORROWER owed LENDER $70,000. LENDER, alleging irregularities in BORROWER's account, demanded payment of the loan and indicated that it would not make any further loans unless BORROWER assigned to LENDER all accounts receivable, caused guarantees to be executed, and delivered security agreements. BORROWER complied and requested additional financing. LENDER refused, and thereafter BORROWER was declared bankrupt. BOR-

ROWER sued LENDER for fraudulent misrepresentation (and other theories), claiming that at the time LENDER made its demands, it knew it would not lend additional funds.

Decision For BORROWER, on the basis of fraudulent misrepresentation. LENDER misrepresented that it might make future loans when it knew it would not. The court awarded $2,100,015.50 to the plaintiffs: $1 million in general damages, $100,000 for emotional distress, $1 million in punitive damages against LENDER, and $15.50 in punitive damages against the loan officer.

Case C

Facts LENDER, which had a long-term relationship with BORROWER, responded to credit inquiries from an automobile dealership financing company. LENDER indicated that at various times the dealership maintained certain balances, was current on its loans, had not overdrawn its account, and that LENDER anticipated funds to be deposited. These responses were not accurate and were apparently made by LENDER for its own advantage to keep the dealership as a going concern so LENDER could obtain the proceeds from the sale of vehicles in which it had a security interest. The financing company, in reliance on the misrepresentations by LENDER, provided a facility to the dealership, ultimately suffered losses, and sued LENDER for fraudulent misrepresentation.

Decision For Financing Company, based on fraudulent misrepresentation. LENDER had made misstatements of material fact, which it knew to be false, with the intent to deceive the financing company. The financing company was damaged as a result of its justifiable reliance on those statements.

PRACTICAL CONSIDERATIONS

- There is no liability for fraudulent misrepresentation if what is represented is true; so be truthful.
- Avoid even the appearance of *scienter*. Never let it be said that you intended to deceive another.

- Confirm the accuracy of your representations if you are not sure. A disregard for the truth may be considered *scienter*.
- Be cautious in what you tell or write to customers.
- Be cautious when responding to credit inquiries.

Chapter Five

Nonfraudulent Misrepresentation

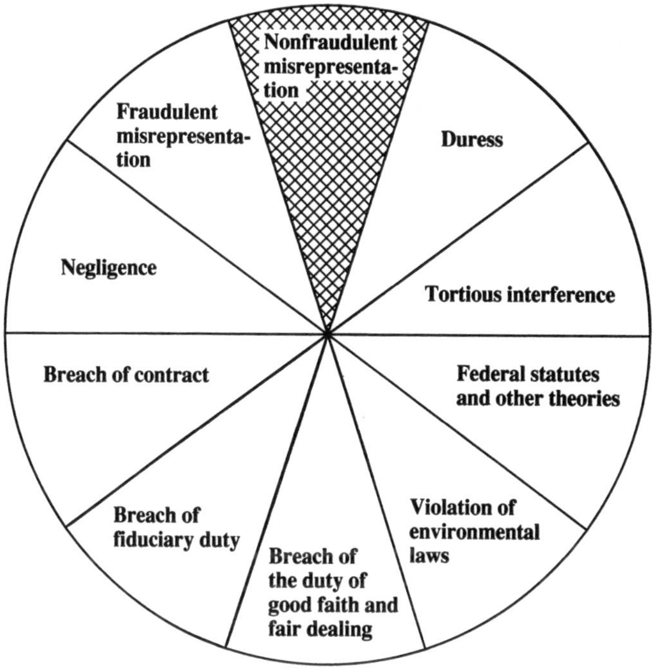

The law will provide a remedy for a person who is harmed by the careless misrepresentation of another.

DEFINITION

Nonfraudulent (sometimes referred to as "negligent" or "innocent") *misrepresentation* is the false representation of a material fact, carelessly made, that is justifiably relied on by and causes damage to another.

ELEMENTS

To prove nonfraudulent misrepresentation the plaintiff must show

- A false representation of a
- Material
- Fact,
- Carelessly made, and
- Justifiable reliance by and
- Damage resulting to another.

DISCUSSION

Assume that when purchasing a used car, you relied on the seller's statement that it had never been in an accident. After the purchase you learned that, in fact, the car had been damaged. The seller's son was the driver at the time and never told the seller, and the seller never exercised the care to check with the son. You could claim nonfraudulent misrepresentation: the representation of fact was false, it was material, it was carelessly made, you justifiably relied on it and were damaged. Even though *fraudulent* misrepresentation may not exist, because there was no knowledge of the falsity and intent to deceive (*scienter*), there may still be liability for the misrepresentation if the representation was carelessly made. The theory of nonfraudulent misrepresentation requires the same elements as fraudulent misrepresentation except that *scienter* is replaced by "carelessness."

DAMAGES

Generally, an agreement induced by nonfraudulent misrepresentation is voidable. The plaintiff may rescind the agreement, receive back what was paid, and be relieved of any obligations. The plaintiff may recover damages, limited to "out-of-pocket" damages actually suffered, not including lost profits. Punitive or exemplary damages are not available.

ILLUSTRATIVE HOLDINGS

Lenders have been held liable for

- Failing to exercise reasonable care in making a promise that the bank would lend on purchase orders received by a corporation.
- Failing to disclose zoning irregularities shown on a plan (purchased by the mortgagors for the purpose of verifying the proper location of the house being purchased).

EXAMPLES

Case A

Facts A loan officer told three individuals that LENDER would make a loan to a corporation (to be formed by them) based on purchase orders to be received by the corporation. Thereafter, the corporation was formed and borrowed $35,000 from LENDER, which was secured by purchased equipment and guaranteed by the three individuals. When this sum was nearly exhausted, the corporate BORROWER desired to obtain the previously discussed loan, which was to be based on its purchase orders. Since their loan officer was on vacation, representatives of BORROWER, in an effort to obtain the funds, visited the president of LENDER, who said the proposed loan was "the most asinine bit of financing" he had ever seen in his life. When he was told that the loan officer had agreed to it, he said, "I don't give a . . . damn who [said] it; you're not getting a damn cent out of this bank." BORROWER subsequently went out of business, and when LENDER sued the guarantors for the deficiency, they counterclaimed with allegations of nonfraudulent misrepresentation.

Decision For the Guarantors. The court held

> where one makes a statement with knowledge that the statement is required for a serious purpose, and that it is made for the benefit of another person, who is expected to rely upon it and may be damaged if it is false, the person making such statement is under a duty to the person expected to rely upon it, to exercise reasonable care that the statement is correct. Failure to exer-

cise reasonable care under such circumstances is . . . [nonfraudulent] misrepresentation.

Case B

Facts BORROWER applied for a residential mortgage loan. LENDER required and ordered, for the account of BORROWER, a plot plan to verify that the location of the house on the lot complied with the town's zoning laws. At the closing, BORROWER asked to see the plan. The mortgage officer said that it was not in the file but would be sent to BORROWER. When BORROWER received the plan, after closing, it showed violations of the zoning law. BORROWER sued LENDER for nonfraudulent misrepresentation for failing to disclose the irregularities.

Decision For BORROWER. LENDER was careless in failing to disclose the plan to BORROWER, for which they had paid, and that the LENDER had in its possession at the time of closing. The judge found that BORROWER would not have purchased the property if BORROWER had had the information. The court held, "The conduct and words of the [loan officer] who handled the . . . closing amounted to a representation to the [BORROWER], negligently made, that the plot plan disclosed no irregularities and that [BORROWER] could safely close without having seen it."

PRACTICAL CONSIDERATIONS

- Even without "an intent to deceive" (*scienter*) there can be liability for a misrepresentation if there is carelessness.
- Be cautious in communicating information that you know will be relied on.
- Check your facts and your authority to communicate before you make any representations to a customer or respond to a credit inquiry.

Chapter Six

Duress

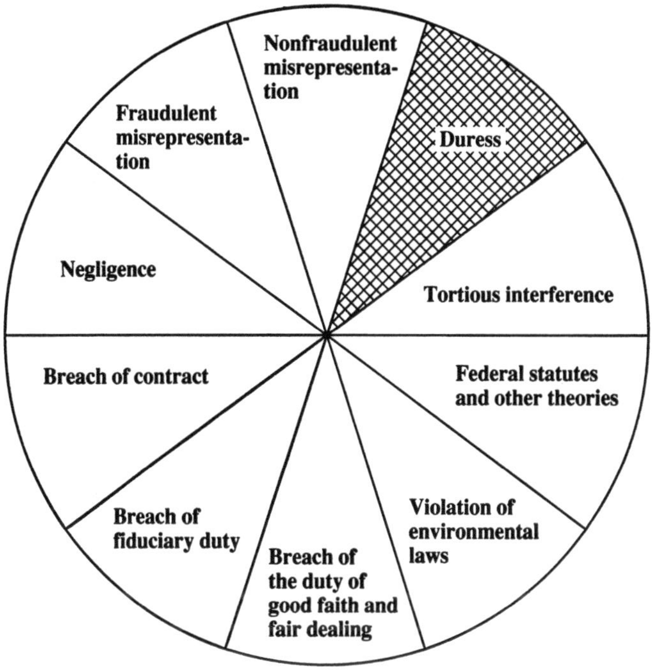

When one is coerced into acting, the act is not that person's free will. Since a contract must be entered into voluntarily, an agreement made under duress will not be enforced.

DEFINITION

Duress is the use of improper threats or acts that coerce a person to act against his or her will.

ELEMENTS

To prove duress the plaintiff must show

- An improper act or threat that
- Overcame the plaintiff's free will and
- Caused the plaintiff to make an agreement.

DISCUSSION

Assume you enter into an agreement to buy a used car from your boss because you were told that if you did not buy it, you would not get a raise. When you default on one of your monthly payments, your boss sues you for breach of contract. You may defend the action by alleging duress. Your boss exerted an improper threat that overcame your free will, causing you to make the agreement. Duress (sometimes called "economic duress" or "business coercion") exists when one party does or threatens to do an act that that party has no legal right to do and the act or threat precludes the other party (the "victim") from exercising free will, causing the victim to do something out of fear that the victim is not legally bound to do.

The court will consider, subjectively, all the facts—including the age, background, experience, and relationship of the parties—to determine if the victim was actually deprived of free will. From the same "threat," for example, a strong, experienced businessperson may not be deprived of free will, whereas a weaker, inexperienced person may be so deprived.

Duress should be distinguished from the actions of a lender asserting its rights under a loan document or engaging in hard bargaining, neither of which involve a wrongful act or threat. Duress may be asserted as a defense to an action or, affirmatively, to rescind an agreement. Some courts have allowed duress to constitute the basis of an independent action for damages.

DAMAGES

Upon a showing that the plaintiff entered into an agreement as a result of duress, the plaintiff may avoid (rescind) the agreement, receive back what was paid, and be relieved of any obligations. The plaintiff may, under certain circumstances and in certain states, recover compensatory or punitive damages.

ILLUSTRATIVE HOLDINGS

Lenders have been held liable for

- Threatening to declare a default, bankrupt the debtor, and padlock its door unless the borrower made certain management decisions.
- Refusing to provide financing to its borrower unless the borrower paid an unrelated debt to an unrelated third party.

EXAMPLES

Case A

Facts The *Farah* case, discussed in Chapter 4, with reference to the theory of fraudulent misrepresentation, also involved allegations of other theories of lender liability, one of which was duress. After reviewing the facts in *Farah*, the court observed

> Duress may be evidenced when a threatening party acts oppressively to further his own economic interest. . . . Economic duress [business coercion] may be evidenced by forcing a victim to choose between distasteful and costly situations, i.e., bow to duress or face bankruptcy, loss of credit rating, or loss of profits from a venture.

The court was referring to the warnings ("threats") to FMC made on behalf of the lenders: a letter stating that the banks would not grant a waiver of the change of management clause if Farah was elected CEO but would consider a waiver if someone else was elected and the threat that counsel would bankrupt the company and padlock it the next day.

Decision For FMC, the BORROWER. The court held that the threats constituted duress. The loan was not in default at the time the creditor implied it would accelerate the loan pursuant to the management change clause. The lenders could have waited until Farah's election, which would have constituted a default, but there were no circumstances to authorize the manner in which the warnings were made. FMC undertook new obligations (not to have Farah elected CEO) as a result of duress.

Case B

Facts LENDER issued its commitment to BORROWER for construction of a housing project, and BORROWER agreed to pay LENDER a fee. After the commitment was issued and the BORROWER had expended considerable money on the planning stages of the project, LENDER demanded an additional fee as compensation for making the loan. LENDER owed $16,000 to a third party, which was willing to accept $12,000 in settlement of the debt. LENDER refused to close with BORROWER unless BORROWER paid the $12,000 debt to the third party. BORROWER paid the $12,000, closed its loan with LENDER, and then sued LENDER for the return of the $12,000 on the theory of duress.

Decision For BORROWER. The court held that LENDER deprived BORROWER of its free will by forcing BORROWER to make payments due to economic compulsion. BORROWER did not voluntarily pay the $12,000 but did so to close its loan. The court noted that if BORROWER had sued LENDER at the time of the wrongful act (instead of paying the $12,000), its loss, due to delay, would have been far greater.

PRACTICAL CONSIDERATIONS

- Do not threaten unless you have a clear right to do so under the terms of the loan documents (for example, the right to call a loan upon the occurrence of an event of default).
- Do not threaten, even if you have the right to do so, unless you intend to follow through.
- An improper demand that an existing borrower execute documents for your institution's benefit (for example, a new note, mortgage, security agreement, form UCC-1) may constitute duress if you deprive the borrower of any meaningful choice.
- Communication to a customer informing the customer of something you have a legal right to do (under the terms of the loan documents or by law) is not an improper threat.

Chapter Seven

Tortious Interference

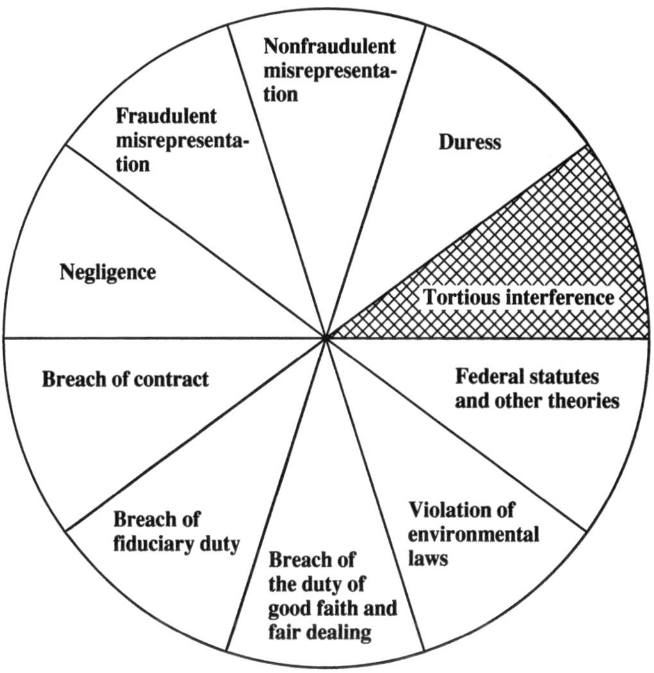

The law protects the sanctity of contracts and will hold a person responsible for interfering with an existing contract or a prospective contractual relationship.

DEFINITION

Tortious interference (with contract) is the intentional and improper interference with the performance of a contract or a prospective contractual relationship by causing a person not to perform in accordance with the terms of the contract or not to enter into the relationship.

ELEMENTS

To prove tortious interference, the plaintiff must show

- The existence of a valid contract or prospective economic advantage.
- The intentional and improper interference with that contract or prospective contractual relationship.
- Damages to the plaintiff caused by the interference.

DISCUSSION

Assume you had an employment contract with your institution. Another lender, aware of your contract, offered you more money to leave your institution to work for it. If you left, your institution may sue the other for tortious interference with your contract.

Tortious interference applies when a person acts with an improper motive or intent to interfere with another's contracts or relationships. The theory has been extended from interference with contracts and prospective contracts (business relations) to interference with corporate governance, when the lender interfered with the corporate management process.

DAMAGES

The successful plaintiff may recover compensatory damages, that is, what the plaintiff would have been entitled to had the terms of the contract been performed or the relationship completed, and, possibly, punitive damages.

ILLUSTRATIVE HOLDINGS

Lenders have been held liable for

- Interfering with a contract between buyer and seller when lender, knowing of a nonencumbrance clause in the contract, induced buyer to violate the clause.
- Exercise of control and domination, forcing concessions from the borrower which ultimately caused its insolvency.
- Using wrongful threats to exercise rights over a borrower, its business activities, and its corporate governance.

EXAMPLES

Case A

Facts Seller agreed to sell a business to BORROWER. The agreement of sale prohibited BORROWER from encumbering the assets (without the consent of seller) until BORROWER had paid seller in full. After the closing of the sale, but before seller was paid, BORROWER applied to LENDER for a $100,000 loan and delivered to LENDER a copy of the purchase agreement containing the prohibition. LENDER made the loan and, without seller's approval, took a security interest in the assets of BORROWER. BORROWER defaulted on the loan, and LENDER claimed the collateral. Seller was required to provide a letter of credit for $100,000 to free the collateral and continue the business, which letter of credit was later drawn on. Seller sued LENDER on the grounds of intentional interference with its contractual relationship.

Decision For Seller. The court found the existence of a valid contractual relationship, knowledge of that contractual relationship by LENDER, and LENDER's intentional and improper interference, causing a breach of the relationship and damages resulting to the seller.

Case B

Facts A workout plan prepared by LENDER required (1) the president of BORROWER to take a 50 percent reduction in salary, (2) a replacement of BORROWER's accountant with one chosen by LENDER, and (3) approval by LENDER of all payments BORROWER desired to make. The court found that the LENDER refused to make payments due by BORROWER, prepared a memorandum containing a "13-point program" to salvage whatever possible, and suggested that the locks be changed on BORROWER's premises. Testimony from BORROWER indicated that LENDER created very severe operating problems and that BORROWER was forced to operate without knowing whether money was available, since LENDER would not tell BORROWER. BORROWER sued LENDER for wrongful interference with its business relationships.

Decision For BORROWER. Based on the evidence, LENDER wrongfully interfered with the business relationships of BORROWER.

Case C

Facts In the *Farah* case (referred to in Chapter 4, in reference to the theory of fraudulent misrepresentation, and in Chapter 6, in reference to the theory of duress), the lender threatened acceleration if Farah was reinstated as CEO and arranged to have individuals with close ties to the lender elected to the board and as CEO. FMC, the BORROWER, as part of its lender liability suit, also claimed the theory of interference with its corporate governance.

Decision For FMC, the BORROWER. The threats made by the lenders that constituted duress also constituted wrongful interference in the BORROWER's corporate governance. The court held

> The lenders interfered with FMC's business relations, its election of directors and officers. . . . FMC was entitled to have its affairs managed by competent directors and officers who would maintain a high degree of undivided loyalty to the company. . . . the interference compelled the election of directors and officers whose particular business judgment and inexperience and whose divided loyalty . . . resulted in injury to FMC. The interference by the lenders was done willfully, intentionally, and without just cause or excuse.

PRACTICAL CONSIDERATIONS

- The line between sound loan administration and interference, especially in troubled loans, is not always clear. Be cautious.
- Suggestions to a borrower are permissible; directives may not be.
- A justifiable business interest does not grant an absolute right to interfere with a contractual relationship between or among others.
- Control of a borrower or its business may give rise to allegations of tortious interference.

Chapter Eight

Breach of Fiduciary Duty

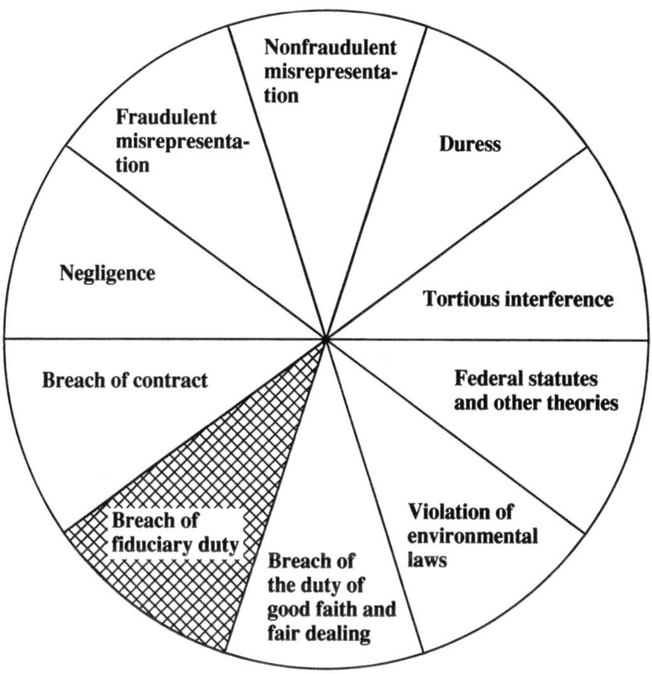

The law recognizes that special relationships impose special standards of conduct. Failure to comply with the required standard of conduct will afford the injured party a remedy.

DEFINITION

A *fiduciary* is one of the parties in a special relationship involving trust and confidence known as *fiduciary relationship*. The existence of the fiduciary relationship imposes on the fiduciary a "fiduciary duty," which requires exercise of the utmost loyalty and good faith.

ELEMENTS

The courts will examine any of the following factors to determine the existence of a fiduciary relationship:

- The acting of one person for another.
- The having and exercising of influence over one person by another.
- The placing of confidence by one person in another.
- The dominance of one person over another.
- The inequality of the parties.
- The dependence of one person on another.

Failure by the fiduciary to exercise the utmost loyalty and good faith is a breach of the fiduciary duty.

DISCUSSION

Common fiduciary relationships involve lawyer and client, director of a corporation and the corporation, partner and his or her other partners, trustee and the beneficiary of the trust. As a general rule, a lender and borrower do not have a fiduciary relationship when their relationship is only one of creditor and debtor. However, special circumstances may give rise to the existence of a fiduciary relationship and the imposition of the fiduciary duty on the lender; for example, the relationship may be found to exist where the lender controls the borrower's business or gives business or financial advice that is relied on by the borrower. The fiduciary duty may even be imposed where the borrower merely perceived the relationship to be one of trust and confidence.

The fiduciary duty is the highest form of a duty. Once it is imposed on a lender, the lender is required to make *all* its decisions in the best interest of a borrower (even if such decisions are not in the interest of the lender), to disclose to the borrower material and confidential information, and to refrain from self-dealing.

DAMAGES

A lender, deemed to be a fiduciary, who breaches its fiduciary duty may be liable for plaintiff's compensatory damages and, possibly, for punitive damages.

ILLUSTRATIVE HOLDINGS

Lenders have been held liable for breach of fiduciary duty when

- Lender advised its borrower to enter into a merger agreement and failed to keep its promise that it would then release personal guarantees.
- Lender induced borrower to act for lender's benefit when, for many years prior thereto, lender acted as financial advisor to borrower and borrower relied on lender's advice.

EXAMPLES

Case A

Facts LENDER made a loan to BORROWER that was guaranteed by plaintiffs, the principal shareholders of BORROWER. LENDER promised to release the plaintiffs from their guarantees if BORROWER merged with another company. After the merger, the new company did not do well, and LENDER refused to release the guarantees. The plaintiffs-guarantors sued LENDER, alleging several theories including breach of fiduciary duty.

Decision For Plaintiffs. The court held that there was substantial evidence of at least a quasi-fiduciary relationship, including plaintiff's perception of a very close relationship with a loan officer, implicit reliance on the loan officer's advice concerning the merger, and the loan officer's sharing of confidential information. Once having established the existence of the fiduciary duty, the court found that LENDER, by failing to release the guarantees, breached its duty to BORROWER.

Case B

Facts BORROWER was a customer of LENDER for approximately 23 years. LENDER's officers and directors had been BORROWER's financial advisors, and BORROWER had been told repeatedly of their friendship for him and had relied on their advice. He believed that LENDER would not take financial advantage of him. LENDER requested a mortgage from BORROWER to secure an existing indebtedness and told BORROWER that the mortgage was required to satisfy the banking department and that LENDER would not foreclose. It did. BORROWER sued LENDER.

Decision For BORROWER. The court held that a relationship of trust and confidence existed and stated

> Where it is alleged a bank has acted as the financial advisor of one of its depositors for many years, and that the [BORROWER] has relied upon such advice . . . a confidential relationship . . . does exist . . . and . . . the bank is subject to the rules applying to confidential relations in general.

PRACTICAL CONSIDERATIONS

- A purely debtor-creditor relationship between the borrower and lender is not a special relationship, and the lender is not a fiduciary.
- A fiduciary relationship may be found and the fiduciary duty imposed when there is actually a special relationship based on trust and confidence or when the borrower perceives such a relationship.
- Adherence at all times to the precepts of good faith and fair dealing may avoid liability even if the fiduciary relationship is found to exist.

Chapter Nine

Breach of the Duty of Good Faith and Fair Dealing

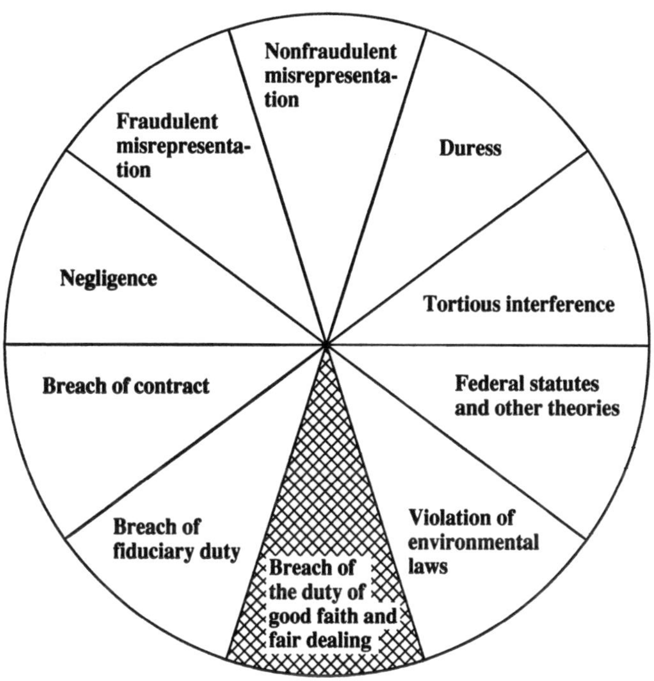

The duty of good faith and fair dealing, in the performance of contracts, requires that each party cooperate with the other party and do nothing to deprive the other from the other's reasonable expectations.

DEFINITION

Good faith means honesty in fact. One in good faith will not take unfair advantage of another. *Bad faith* is conduct that violates community standards of reasonableness, fairness, or decency.

ELEMENTS

There are three sources of the duty of good faith that, collectively, have the effect of imposing the duty of good faith in all contracts: traditional contract law, traditional tort law, and the Uniform Commercial Code.

Contract Law

Every contract imposes, by implication, on each party a duty of good faith and fair dealing in its performance and its enforcement.

Tort Law

If a party breaches the implied duty of good faith, that party may not only be liable for breach of contract but may also be liable for damages for an independent tort.

Uniform Commercial Code (the "UCC")

Every contract or duty within the UCC imposes an obligation of good faith in its performance or enforcement. In addition, the UCC requires a belief, in good faith, that the prospect of payment of performance is impaired before a lender may accelerate "at will" or when it deems itself "insecure."

DISCUSSION

The obligation of good faith and fair dealing has long existed in the law. It is an *implied* duty; therefore, the words "good faith" or "fair dealing" need not be expressed in the contract. Without this duty, a party could render its promises meaningless by sabotaging its own agreements. For example, if you signed a contract to buy a house, subject to you obtaining a mortgage commitment, you are required, in good faith, to apply for the commitment, pay the appropriate fees, and cooperate with the lender. To hold otherwise would allow you, if you changed your mind about the purchase and then did not apply for the commitment or did not pay the lender's fees or did not cooperate with the lender, to claim you were excused from the obligation to purchase because you did not obtain the commitment.

Now, plaintiffs are using the duty of good faith and fair dealing as the basis for lender liability actions. Lenders do not usually engage in forms of conduct that are obviously in bad faith. However, courts are finding that the failure to give reasonable notice to a borrower may be deemed a breach of the duty of good faith and fair dealing. While lenders must perform all of the terms of their contracts in good faith, they are particularly vulnerable in two areas:

1. When the lender has the right to exercise discretion; for example, to advance funds in its discretion, or to accelerate "at will" or when it feels "insecure."
2. When the lender varies from an established course of conduct; for example, continuously accepting late payments and then suddenly deciding to accelerate.

DAMAGES

The successful plaintiff may recover compensatory damages, as in a breach of contract action. In certain circumstances, punitive damages may be available if the wrongful act is a tort.

ILLUSTRATIVE HOLDINGS

Contract Law

A lender was held liable for $7.5 million in damages for breach of the implied duty of good faith by failing to give notice to the borrower before refusing to advance funds under a loan agreement.

Tort Law

A lender was held liable, due to the failure of a bank officer to notify a superior of modified loan terms, when the lender mistakenly, without notice to the borrower, accelerated the maturity of the debt.

UCC

A lender was held liable when it terminated the borrower's credit arrangement, without fair notice, when it knew the borrower's business depended on it.

EXAMPLES

Case A: Contract Law

Facts KMC, a wholesale grocer, entered into a financing agreement with Irving Trust Company (Irving) whereby Irving agreed to provide a line of credit, in its discretion, up to $3.5 million. The loan was due on demand and was secured by all of KMC's accounts receivable and inventory. The proceeds of all of KMC's receivables were required to be deposited into a "blocked account" to which only Irving had access.

KMC requested an advance of $800,000, which was available under its line. Irving, which was fully collateralized, refused, and eventually KMC was forced to liquidate its business.

KMC, in its suit against Irving (*KMC Co.* v. *Irving Trust Co.*, [1985]), alleged, among other things, that Irving breached its implied duty of good faith and fair dealing by terminating the line without notice. Irving defended by arguing that since the line was due on demand and that because advances were discretionary, it could terminate the line at any time.

Decision For KMC, the BORROWER. The jury awarded KMC $7.5 million in damages on the theory that Irving breached its implied duty of good faith and fair dealing by not giving KMC notice of its intention to terminate the line.

The court noted that even though the obligation of KMC was evidenced by a demand note (to which the obligation of good faith under the UCC does not apply), provisions in the loan agreements indicated that the parties did not actually intend the instrument to be due on demand. The existence of financial covenants and events of default were held to be inconsistent with the demand nature of the note and required that Irving exercise discretion, in good faith.

The court held

> The record clearly established that a medium-sized company . . . such as KMC could not operate without outside financing. Thus, the literal interpretation of the financing agreement . . . as supplemented by the "blocked account" mechanism, would leave KMC's continued existence entirely at the whim or mercy of Irving, absent an obligation of good faith performance. . . . Logically, at such time as Irving might wish to curtail financing KMC, as was its right under the agreement, this obligation to act in good faith would require a period of notice to KMC to allow it a reasonable opportunity to seek alternative financing.

Case B: Tort Law

Facts BORROWER, operator of a restaurant, borrowed $3,500 to buy an ice machine and to pay property taxes. LENDER received a security interest in the ice machine, inventory, and receivables. The note was a time note due in a single payment of principal and interest. BORROWER, thereafter, negotiated with a certain loan officer to have the note converted to an installment note. That officer was going out of town and told BORROWER that another loan officer would handle the loan.

The replacement loan officer knew nothing of the prior negotiations, believed the note to be in jeopardy, and declared it immediately due. LENDER then offset the amount due against the BORROWER's checking account, leaving a balance of $1.65. No notice was given to BORROWER, who learned of the offset when its checks bounced. BORROWER sued the LENDER for tortious breach of the duty of good faith.

Decision For BORROWER. The court found that LENDER breached its obligation to act in good faith and that it acted in reckless disregard of the BORROWER's rights. In determining the note to be in jeopardy, LENDER did not attempt to establish whether BORROWER was intending to leave the community or any other information to support a threat to the repayment of the note. In such a case, BORROWER may recover punitive damages as well as compensatory damages.

Case C: Uniform Commercial Code

Facts BORROWER, after obtaining several smaller loans from LENDER over a period of several years, executed a $25,000 demand note and entered into a commercial line of credit agreement to be used to finance BORROWER's painting business. Several months after entering into the credit agreement, LENDER terminated the arrangement. As a result of the lack of funds, BORROWER's automobile was repossessed (and, in the process, BORROWER on the complaint of LENDER was arrested and jailed), his business collapsed, he lost four vehicles and his home, he filed for bankruptcy, his wife suffered emotional problems, and then the couple separated.

Decision For BORROWER, for compensatory damages of $100,000. The court held that LENDER's actions terminating the line without notice to the BORROWER and without an effort to negotiate alternative solutions were not taken in good faith (which was implied in the credit agreement). The court noted that when BORROWER's line was abruptly shut off, he was not in default and his overall position had not changed significantly, especially as LENDER did not first register complaints to him or ask him to alter his conduct in some manner. The "demand" nature of the note could not be read literally in the context of the agreement of the parties.

PRACTICAL CONSIDERATIONS

- Because the duty of good faith and fair dealing is implied in *all* contracts, be constantly aware of the reasonableness, fairness, and decency of your words and actions.
- It is not safe to assume that because you have a demand instrument, a court will not require reasonable notice to the borrower as part of your duty of good faith and fair dealing, especially if there are docu-

ments or arrangements tending to be inconsistent with the "demand" character of the instrument.

- Make sure your file shows that decisions concerning discretionary actions were made in good faith, especially refusals to advance, or accelerating "at will," or when you feel "insecure."
- Do not engage in a course of conduct not in accordance with the loan documents. If you do, then do not suddenly revert to the strict application of the documents. A court may find that your inconsistent conduct takes precedence over the loan documents.
- Even if not obligated to so do, give reasonable notice to your borrowers, whenever you can, *if* your position will not be harmed.

PART

II

AVOIDING OR MINIMIZING EXPOSURE TO LIABILITY

Chapter Ten

The Basics

There is no way to ensure that your institution will not be sued. The right to sue of a person who believes he or she has been harmed is one of the fundamental rights we all enjoy. You can and should, however, do everything possible to minimize or avoid the risks of lender liability.

Three fundamental behaviors, if practiced consistently, may decrease the risk of allegations of lender liability:

- Be truthful.
- Be fair.
- Use counsel.

TRUTH

By being truthful you establish customer relationships based on trust, and a trusting relationship is less likely to deteriorate into a hostile one. A truthful relationship makes for a more comfortable relationship; you will not have to wonder what you told that particular borrower the last time.

From a legal position, the existence of truth eliminates one of the necessary elements of several theories of liability. For example, fraudulent and nonfraudulent misrepresentation each require the element of a *misstatement* of fact. If the truth is represented, there can be no misstatement.

Be truthful by being accurate, and be truthful by keeping your promises to do what you said you were going to do. This course of conduct will avoid allegations of breach of contract and eliminate allegations of fraudulent misrepresentation when a threat is made to a borrower.

Truth should be tempered with diplomacy and tact. Often, the truth is not what a customer wants to hear. When delivering less-than-welcome news, try to deliver it delicately to avoid the appearance of the lack of good faith. When bad news is delivered harshly, you not only risk allegations of bad faith but may induce an unhappy borrower to become a litigious one.

FAIRNESS

Fairness is related to truth but is not the same. One can be honest in fact but not fair. The loan officer who suddenly calls a demand loan without giving the borrower any notice (and therefore an opportunity to refinance) may be completely within his or her rights under the loan documents but may be held to have treated the borrower unfairly.

You may be aware of many clauses in your set of loan documents that may be used as the basis for claims of technical defaults. If, however, those technical defaults are called after a contrary course of conduct or suddenly, the court may find that you were not dealing fairly and in good faith.

Allegations of lack of good faith and unfairness may be used as an independent basis for lender liability or may be considered evidence in support of other theories. The popular perception that lenders are the stronger and borrowers the weaker parties may tend to make it more difficult to defend against allegations of unfairness.

Ask, "Can I legally (and economically) afford to be fairer?" If the answer is no, do what you have to do. If the answer is yes, perhaps you will actually help the borrower, and, if not, you will have (possibly) removed the grounds for an allegation of breach of the duty of good faith and fair dealing.

COUNSEL

You are being thrown into a game with new and changing rules. While you should be familiar with the area of lender liability, it is unfair to assume you are an expert in the legal niceties of the subject. Counsel can help. Solicit advice early. Request an opinion when you are in doubt or uncomfortable. You should not feel that lender liability decisions are your call alone.

Chances are that counsel will have dealt with the same or similar issues before and will be able to offer immediate guidance. If the question is one that requires legal research, the delay is usually worth avoidance of the potential risk.

As you continue to deal with counsel, you will become more comfortable with the subject of lender liability and will find yourself seeking advice less frequently and then, probably, only to confirm your opinions. But remember, when in doubt—ask.

Chapter Eleven

In Practice

Your working relationship with the borrower affords you the opportunity to avoid or minimize the risks of lender liability. The suggestions that follow range from the obvious to the subtle, from the general to the specific, and from first contact to closing, during administration and afterward.

You are a professional. Hold yourself out as a professional. Treat your borrowers fairly and, when necessary, firmly. Don't hesitate to say no. How many times have borrowers asked you to waive a closing requirement, to give them a few more days, or to otherwise accommodate them? If you agree with the requests, you may please them, or save them a little money, or cause the transaction to take place a little sooner—but you may have increased your risk of lender liability.

Before lender liability lawsuits were so common, you could afford to be extremely generous. After all, all you could lose was principal and interest (and, possibly, your job). Today, you simply cannot afford to be magnanimous without first considering the risks. It is more important than ever that your institution's business and legal policies be followed.

On the other hand, recognize that by virtue of your position, to your borrowers, you wield enormous power. Be sensitive not to abuse that power. At all stages of the relationship consider your customer's needs and act reasonably, but be cautious and conservative and protective of your institution's position. Start a program of defensive measures from the onset of the customer relationship. Consider adopting the following suggestions as standard practices. At first they may seem forced and strange, but as they are incorporated as part of your routine, they will become more natural.

MAKE AND MAINTAIN GOOD FILES

Create files as if every document was going to be read by hostile eyes. Allowing bad information to be in your file is like providing the hangman with the noose.

Be Factual

The file should contain only accurate statements of facts. Do not allow notes containing your opinions as to the questionable parentage or lack of intellect of a borrower to be found. Regardless of their merits, such opinions will not impress a court with your professionalism or fairness.

Be Complete

An incomplete file is not credible. All relevant information should be there. If you called on a borrower, there should be a call report. If you requested financials, a copy of the letter should be in your file. Generally, copies of all relevant correspondence, memos of telephone calls, minutes of meetings, as well as all financial information should be in the file. Do not, however, overload a file with extraneous or irrelevant information that will make the file confusing.

PUT IT IN WRITING!

Why Put It in Writing?

A written document serves two major purposes in a business transaction. First, it preserves a record. In a typical loan transaction, it is not possible to remember all of one's agreements; the volume is simply too great. With any number of loan files active at the same time, it is not possible for you to keep track of the various loan terms, no less the covenants, ratios, special conditions, and like matters, for all of your customers. Similarly, never rely on a customer's oral promises or statements. Get them in writing. Memories are weak, and borrowers' memories become weaker the more their interests diverge from yours. Second, written agreements are probably the best evidence available in the event of litigation. More reliable than a party's memory, more accurate than a witness, and more persuasive to a judge or jury is a document signed by the party denying his or her agreement.

There is still another advantage. Once a signed document is in your file it has a deterrent effect. A borrower who has signed a loan agreement is less likely to rush to dispute (or to litigate) what was said or intended if the borrower knows you have a copy of the agreement.

Silence Is Golden

The corollary to "put it in writing" is, of course, do not make any oral promises to a borrower or potential borrower. Try not to tell the borrower, over lunch, that you will obtain the requested loan, or assure the borrower of the desired increase in the line, or that the loan will close at a certain rate. It may not be easy to refrain from such comments, particularly if you have a close existing relationship or if you are trying to establish a new relationship. After all, the ability to make these types of representations reflects on your stature and power as a loan officer. Do not do it. Hedge. Tell the customer that the bank will consider the request, or that you will see what you can do. You will thus avoid placing the institution in the position of defending against allegations of breach of contract, negligence, misrepresentation, or other theories of lender liability.

Do not try to support or mitigate the meaning of any terms of the loan documents by telling the borrower that the language is "standard" or that the lender will never do this or that, or that the borrower has nothing to worry about. This time, the borrower's memory becomes elephantlike. The borrower who could not remember to pay on the first of the month will never forget your assurance of comfort. At the closing, let counsel respond to the borrower's legal-type questions.

LEGAL COUNSEL

Require the Borrower (and All Guarantors) to Have Counsel

You may be tempted to allow a borrower to proceed with a transaction without counsel when the borrower argues

1. A desire to save the legal fees. (Yes, there might be some savings of legal fees. But consider that this reason is usually used in smaller transactions where the legal fees are relatively small, and while the borrower may save a few dollars, it is you who is taking the risk.)
2. Borrower does not need counsel because the transaction is "boilerplate." (There is no such thing as a "boilerplate transaction.")
3. Borrower does not need counsel because the lender has counsel. (Lender's counsel cannot ethically represent the borrower in most instances.)
4. Borrower does not need counsel because the transaction is a repeat or an extension of an earlier transaction. (If, in fact, the transaction is similar to or an extension or modification of an earlier transaction, the borrower's counsel's time usually will be less and his fees less.)

Borrowers should have counsel to advise and protect them. The participation of borrower's counsel will (usually) make for a more expeditious transaction.

Borrower's Counsel Will Benefit You

The participation of borrower's counsel may insulate you from later claims by an unhappy borrower that the borrower "didn't understand," "wasn't informed," or was told something at closing that was not contained in, or was inconsistent with, the loan documents. Furthermore, having borrower's counsel relieves you of the not unusual and time-consuming burden of walking the borrower through and explaining the loan documents.

The Borrower's Brother-In-Law May Not Be the Best Choice of Counsel.

If borrower has counsel who you feel is not experienced in the area of your transaction, it is not inappropriate to so notify the borrower. Competent counsel on both sides makes for a cleaner and safer transaction.

ATTENDANCE AT CLOSING

All parties should be present at closing if at all possible. It is not a good practice to have documents signed outside of the closing room or by power of attorney.

The Borrower May Not Appreciate What He Is Signing outside the Closing Room

When documents are signed outside of the closing room, you are more vulnerable to claims by a disgruntled borrower that: borrower did not understand the document or thought it was something else, borrower was not represented by counsel, or borrower's lawyer did not advise the borrower as to the document's meaning or contents. These allegations can be transformed into legal actions against the lender based on breach of contract, negligence, fraudulent and nonfraudulent misrepresentation, and other theories. While some of these statements may be patently ridiculous, especially when made by an experienced businessperson, they are made all the time in the course of litigation.

The Documents May Not Be Properly Executed outside the Closing Room

The greatest danger related to execution of documents outside the closing room concerns the issues of authenticity and due execution. The guaranty document signed outside of closing may not, in fact, bear the signature of the absent spouse of the borrower. In addition, in many states, law or custom requires certain formalities to be followed for the proper execution or recording of a document; for example, two witnesses or a particular form of acknowledgment may be required for recording. By permitting your loan documents to be signed outside the closing room you are inviting problems ranging from errors that will merely delay (or abort) the closing to a closed transaction with defective or ineffective documents.

When It Is Unavoidable

In some instances, a necessary party will just not be available to attend the closing. In such cases, when you cannot conveniently adjourn the closing, you may have to agree that a document may be signed outside the closing by a party, or by the party's authorized agent using a power of attorney. You should only so agree if there is an existing customer relationship and the customer's (and, if applicable, the absent party's) character is known to you and you are comfortable; and then only if the absent party's signature is witnessed or acknowledged by the borrower's attorney (or another attorney), as the notary public.

TAKING ACTION

Be smooth. Be steady. Do not rock the boat. If the existing relationship has followed a certain course of conduct that you now wish to change, when possible, do not change suddenly. Give the borrower reasonable notice, particularly if the lender has not objected to or has effectively waived borrower's shortcomings in the past. Such notice is evidence of your good faith and fairness. If you allowed a borrower to be late with payment for the last six months, do not call the note on the second day of the current month. If the borrower has been in default of the required ratios for three months with no comment from the lender, do not suddenly accelerate. It is not difficult for you (or a judge and jury) to imagine that adverse business consequences could result from a sudden change of conduct by a lender.

Demanding

If, for example, you have a demand note in which no notice is required and the borrower has no idea that you intend to demand, give fair notice anyway, *if* you will not be hurt by the delay. It gives the borrower an opportunity to obtain substitute financing without being damaged. If not damaged, the borrower is not likely to allege a theory of lender liability. If your loan documents contain provisions that may be interpreted as inconsistent with the demand nature of the note (events of default, affirmative or negative covenants, or other performance standards), a court may hold that you are required to give reasonable notice, because the instrument is not truly due on demand.

Accelerating

If you have the right to accelerate, the comments made above with reference to demanding generally apply. Give notice, even if you are not required to do so by the terms of the loan documents. A sudden, unexpected acceleration may not be deemed to be fair and in good faith, particularly where the lender is fully secured. If you are relying on an "insecurity" provision in the note or other loan documents, your file should support the basis for your feeling of insecurity.

Terminating

In the *KMC* case (referred to in Chapter 9, with reference to the duty of good faith and fair dealing), the court held that the lender was required to give reasonable notice to the borrower before it terminated its line of credit, even though the note was a demand note and even though the lender had the right to make discretionary advances. In that case, the lender, which was fully secured, suddenly terminated its borrower's line and caused the borrower to go out of business.

If you can do so without risking your position, give reasonable notice before terminating a line or ceasing to make further discretionary advances, even if you are not required to do so by a strict reading of the loan documents. This is especially important if your loan documents contain any provisions not absolutely consistent with the demand character of the debt instrument, such as events of default, affirmative or negative covenants, or other performance standards.

THINK AND ACT DEFENSIVELY

Support the correctness of your actions before you act. Your file should defend, with factual and objective data, the reasons for your conduct (for example, the basis for your notice of default, acceleration, or termination).

The evidence can consist of internal memoranda sent to or from you, correspondence to the borrower, call reports, minutes of meetings, memos to the file, or other similar documentation. Financials, credit reports, and tax returns may all support your decisions and your actions. Take care especially to support any discretionary decisions, actions taken "at will" or because you felt "insecure," or the exercise of any default provisions at your "option." Contemporaneous documents, kept in the ordinary course of administering the loan, may be afforded the most weight by a court if your actions are challenged.

Before you act, ask, Could my words or conduct invite allegations of lender liability? What can I do *now* to support and defend my position?

DO NOT BULLY

Be firm. Be fair. Do not threaten unless you are authorized and prepared to promptly carry out the threat. An act or a threat, even if not improper, may influence a judge's or jury's view of your good faith and fairness. In addition, under the *Farah* decision, a threat that is not carried out may be considered fraudulent as a misstatement of fact. Before you threaten, orally or in writing, check with counsel as to your authority (and, if authorized, as to the form) and put a memo in the file.

DO NOT TRY TO DO IT ALL YOURSELF

Know your strengths and recognize other people's strengths. The focus of your background and experience may be transactional, that is, soliciting customers, analyzing the credit, structuring the transaction, closing, and administration. You may be well qualified in those areas. If, however, the loan is in trouble or in default, are you as qualified in the area of workout? Could you be objective? Could you do what is necessary to *your* customer to protect your institution, or would your relationship with the customer interfere with your ability to act forcibly? Do not hesitate to contact and work with the workout specialist at your institution. That person's knowledge and experience may not necessarily be greater than yours, but his or her objectivity is.

COMMUNICATE CAREFULLY

Take care to be truthful and accurate (and fair) in your communications with your borrower. The borrower may be relying on what you communicate, and erroneous information can lay the foundation for many theories of liability.

When credit inquiries are received concerning your customers, follow the guidelines set forth in the *Statement of Principles for the Exchange of Credit Information* published by Robert Morris Associates and the National Association of Credit Management. Respond factually, request proper identification of the inquirer, and keep the identity of the inquirers and sources confidential. If in doubt about whether to respond or about an appropriate response, seek counsel.

DO NOT CONTROL

Do not control or attempt to control the borrower or its business. "Control" by a lender has a myriad of legal consequences, and all of them are bad.

- Do not control selection of the borrower's board of directors.
- Do not control the borrower's choice of advisors or consultants.
- If your documents contain a management change clause, do not use it as a tool to control selection of management.
- Do not control the business operations of a borrower.
- Do not control the business or finances, or production or disposal of hazardous wastes, of a customer with environmental problems.

Chapter Twelve

In Documentation

When preparing or reviewing loan documents, you may be able to limit exposure to claims of lender liability. Drafting of legal documents is not usually the responsibility of the loan officer, but an awareness and understanding of their meanings will assist you in dealing with borrowers (and counsel) and in protecting your position.

BE CLEAR

Your objective should be the avoidance of ambiguity, confusion, and misunderstanding. After you have written or reviewed a sentence, a paragraph, or a document, ask, "Now that *I* understand the language, will *everyone else* reading these same words have the same understanding?" If the answer is anything but an unequivocal yes!, it needs work. Writing clearly and precisely takes practice and patience.

Do not assume your reader knows what you know. If you are using banking or business terms, define them (for example, "prime" or "borrowing base"). Once you have defined a term or otherwise made its meaning clear, do not hesitate to repeat it. In business or legal communications, repetition is preferable to ambiguity.

Strive to be precise in all of your communications. For those of us not blessed with golden tongues or pens, a routine of drafting and redrafting, editing, and revising will help.

Try to be concise. Review your work product to eliminate unnecessary words and to avoid unnecessary repetition of thoughts. This will cause you to go through a process of selection to find the "right" word that helps you to be precise. Furthermore, the more said, the greater the opportunity for ambiguity, confusion, or misunderstanding.

Keep in mind words of condition that assist in clearly communicating to your reader that you are not absolutely committing or promising (for example, *if*, *when*, *upon*, *subject to*, *on condition that*, *contingent upon*, *might*, *maybe*, *depending upon*, and *supposing*).

BE COMPLETE

Ambiguity, confusion, and misunderstanding (and litigation) can result not only from language that is not clear but also from language or documents that are not complete. By omitting an essential term, phrase, or paragraph from your documents, you may, if you are lucky, end up devoting substantial time and effort to correcting the document (if the borrower cooperates); or, if you are not so lucky, you may have lost the right to incorporate the missing language.

Before you finish your writing or review of a document, ask, "What else should be included in the document (that may not be obvious)?" (for example, prepayment premium or cross-default or cross-collateralization language).

FOCUS ON LEGALLY SENSITIVE DOCUMENTS

Loan officers are usually more intimately involved with certain documents than others. You may be called on to draft or review letters of intent, commitment letters, notices to borrowers, or "waiver letters."

Letters of Intent

Letters of intent are two-edged swords. They are attractive but risky marketing tools. Properly drawn and promptly sent to a proposed borrower, the letter of intent is a form of public relations indicating how responsive the lender can be to the needs of its customer. The customer impressed by the immediate attention of the lender may then be inclined to establish a relationship. The risk involves potential claims by the proposed borrower that the letter "promised" the borrower a loan, or that the borrower or someone else "relied" on the letter, or that they were "induced" to change their position based on the letter. These claims may give rise to allegations of lender liability based on the theories of breach of contract, negligence, fraudulent and nonfraudulent misrepresentation, as well as others.

To a borrower, the purposes of a letter of intent are to set forth the terms of the proposed loan and to offer assurance that the request shall be given attention. To the lender, there are three basic substantive purposes:

- To outline the proposed transaction to assure that the parties have a common understanding.
- To request additional information or items that may be necessary for a proper evaluation.
- To limit legal exposure from any unwanted potential liability.

A properly drawn letter of intent should not obligate the lender, in any manner, to make any loan. The only acceptable legal consequence is the possible imposition on the lender of the obligation to evaluate, in good faith, the borrower's loan request.

To avoid allegations of unintended and unwanted obligations, the letter should not expressly or impliedly promise anything other than (possibly) to consider the loan request and should be emphatic in its message that no other obligation to the proposed borrower is intended or undertaken. Disclaimer language such as the following is appropriate: "This proposal is . . . subject to approval, rejection, or modification by the Lender's Loan Committee, and if a commitment letter is issued, to the terms and conditions thereof . . ." and "This Letter of Intent is not an agreement to lend or to issue a commitment to lend, and should not be relied on by you or any other person for any such purposes."

In some cases, the proposed borrower will request stronger language indicating the likelihood of approval of the transaction. Beware! Consider the request very carefully and accommodate the customer only if you have the authority to do so and the existing relationship warrants it. Try to avoid the issue by suggesting that the form of the letter of intent is a matter of policy and is not subject to material change.

Commitment Letters

Since the commitment letter is usually the first substantive document to be executed and since it describes documents and acts required in the future, it must be precisely, clearly, and completely drawn. While this may seem obvious, it is particularly difficult because the commitment letter is drawn at a point in the transaction when many details are unknown and many terms may still have to be negotiated.

To the borrower, the purpose of the commitment letter is to offer assurance that the loan will be made, subject to the terms of the letter. To the lender, it has three major purposes:

- To bind the parties in accordance with their agreements.
- To set forth those events that may allow the lender to be excused from performance if certain conditions are not met, or to terminate its agreements if otherwise warranted.
- To outline (with sufficient detail to be of use to the parties and counsel) the legal and business steps that must be taken and the legal documents that must be prepared in order to close.

These varied purposes cause the commitment letter to be a paradoxical document. The lender wants to be bound, but not too bound, and it does not want to be bound only by the terms of the commitment letter. Thus the commitment letter, after binding the lender, sets forth (1) conditions, in the nature of escape hatches, that permit bailing out before the closing and (2) events on which the lender can terminate the commitment even if the proposed borrower has complied with the terms of the commitment letter. Example: the letter may include, as conditions to the obligation to lend, receipt of a satisfactory appraisal or receipt of a satisfactory opinion letter from borrower's counsel; and as excuses from performance, that there has been a materially adverse change in the financial condition of the borrower or that all fees and expenses have not been paid.

Consider including, among others, the following as conditions:

1. Receipt of satisfactory evidence that the mortgaged premises (the "Premises") (*a*) are undamaged; (*b*) are in compliance with all building, zoning, and environmental laws, rules, and regulations, and any other applicable laws and regulations and insurance underwriters' requirements and that all applicable permits and/or certificates have been obtained; (*c*) are insured to the satisfaction of lender and that policies of insurance are paid in full; (*d*) are not located in a federally designated flood zone (or that flood insurance satisfactory to the lender is in effect); and (*e*) are free from any environmental issues or problems.

2. Receipt of satisfactory evidence that borrower's assets are unencumbered and undamaged.
3. Receipt of satisfactory evidence that leases, if any, are subordinate to the lien of any proposed mortgage.
4. Receipt of a current survey of the Premises certified to the lender by a licensed surveyor satisfactory to the lender and its counsel.
5. Receipt of an environmental audit in form and substance satisfactory to lender.
6. Receipt of an opinion of borrower's counsel, in form and substance satisfactory to counsel for lender.
7. Receipt and approval by lender's counsel of the form and substance of drafts or photocopies of all documents requested by lender or its counsel, at least five business days prior to closing.
8. Payment of all fees and expenses of lender.
9. Fulfillment of all other requirements set forth in the commitment letter.

Consider including, among others, the following as events upon the happening of which the lender may terminate the commitment:

1. Upon borrower's or any guarantor's failure to fulfill any of the terms of the commitment letter within the time and in the manner provided therein.
2. If any fees and expenses are not paid according to the terms of the commitment letter.
3. If any of the statements or representations made by the borrower or any guarantor are untrue.
4. If the maximum permissible interest rate under any law or government regulations on the date of closing is less than the interest rate stated in the commitment letter; or if prior to closing, any federal, state, or local law becomes effective, or any court, administrative, or regulatory decision is rendered, that may be reasonably interpreted as being adverse to the business interests of the lender.
5. If there is any material, adverse change in the financial condition or affairs of borrower or any guarantor.

Notices (Notice-Letters)

Notices are usually formal communications, in the form of a letter, sent to the borrower by the lender informing the borrower of some matter that has or will have legal consequences. Notices, for example, may be sent to inform the borrower that (1) payment was late (and a late payment fee is due), (2) payment was not received or performance was not rendered on the due date or as required (and there is a period within which to cure), (3) an event of default has occurred, (4) default has occurred, and the lender is electing to accelerate the entire indebtedness, (5) demand for payment of a demand instrument is being made, (6) no further advances will be made, or (7) the line is being terminated or will not be renewed. Because of the serious legal consequences that may result from such notices, great care to their form and substance is advised.

Form If the form of the notice is prescribed in the loan documents, the notice to be sent to the borrower must conform. Usually one or more of the loan documents will contain a clause entitled "Notices" that typically requires all notices to be in writing, and be transmitted in a certain manner (for example, certified or registered mail, return receipt requested), and to a designated address and sets forth the effective date of the notice (for example, the notice is deemed to have been received on the second day after the notice is mailed).

It is imperative to adhere strictly to the terms of any such notice provision; failure to do so may render the notice ineffective. In the best case, you will have lost time; in the worst case, you may have lost legal rights to collect the debt or foreclose on the collateral. If your loan documents do not contain such a notice provision, give *written* notice and transmit it by a means that will generate proof that you sent it and proof that the borrower received it (for example, courier or registered or certified mail, return receipt requested). Verbal notice or notice that does not conform to the requirements of the loan documents or other types of notice should only be given in addition to, and not in lieu of, the prescribed form of (or, if none, written) notice.

If the notice-letter requests action by the borrower (for example, a payment or the curing of a nonpayment default), include the period of time by which the action is required. Set forth the actual date; for example, use "February 1, 1992," not "30 days from the date hereof." The borrower may not know if "30 days" means a "month" and may not know how to calculate the time period (does the borrower count the day your notice is dated as the first day or start counting with the following day?).

Notices, in general, should be factual, brief, and to the point. Deliver the required message and stop. Opinions about the borrower or his behavior are not professional and may indicate a lack of good faith; unwarranted or unauthorized threats may lead to allegations of fraudulent or nonfraudulent misrepresentation or duress.

Substance The "re" or reference portion of the notice-letter should describe the loan transaction or loan document in sufficient detail to avoid any confusion concerning which transaction is the subject of the letter. More detail is necessary if the borrower has several loans or facilities outstanding or available.

In the body of the letter, state the nature of the letter; for example, "This is notice of your default" or "This is notice of our election to accelerate" or "This is demand for." In all cases, assure that the language in your notice-letter tracks the language contained in the loan document provision under which you are asserting your rights.

Inform the borrower of the specific source of your rights: "In accordance with Article XXIII of the Loan Agreement dated January 2, 1992" or "Under the terms of Paragraph 38 of the Security Agreement dated January 2, 1992."

State the exact nature of the breach, the demand, or the action desired; for example, "Your failure to pay interest in the sum of $2,500 due on September 2, 1992"; "Lender hereby demands payment in full of your note dated January 2, 1992"; "Lender has determined that no additional funds shall be advanced."

In notice-letters in which you wish the borrower to take action at a future time:

(*a*) If the loan documents require a certain grace or cure period, make sure you actually afford the borrower that period of time. Use actual dates, not time periods that have to be calculated.

(*b*) If no time period is prescribed in the loan documents, when you can (without jeopardizing your position), give the borrower a *reasonable* period of time, particularly if the borrower's business or property could be harmed by your sudden action. There exists no definition of "reasonable period of time" or "reasonable notice." Presumably, it is sufficient time for a diligent borrower to cure the default (if that is what is requested) or to attempt to refinance or to make other financial arrangements (if demand has been made), as the case may be. In each case, the time period must be determined based on the particular facts involved. If you were sending a demand notice or notice of termination of a line of credit, for example, and wished to give the borrower an opportunity to make other arrangements, a reasonable period of time would be longer than if you were sending a notice of a payment default, in which the time period to cure would be relatively short. Ask, "How much time may I allow the borrower without jeopardizing my position?" Then give the borrower as much notice as you safely and reasonably can.

Since notices are so factually intensive and may have serious legal consequences, it is prudent to have counsel review your notice-letters.

Waivers (Waiver-Letters)

Borrowers desiring to be relieved from the strict application of the terms of the loan documents may request that you "waive" certain rights or entitlements that exist for the benefit or protection of your institution. To "waive" something is a technical and legal act fraught with possibly adverse consequences. A *waiver* is the relinquishment, or giving up, of a legal right. Usually, you will not actually intend to give up any of your rights but merely to forebear, in a particular instance, from asserting the right. Use of the word *waiver* in your letter may be construed as something other than or broader than intended. Therefore, extreme care should be exercised when responding to requests for waivers.

Always require that any requests be in writing and specifically refer to the provision(s) of the loan documents from which the borrower seeks relief. This procedure will focus the issues for the parties and help assure that your response will address only provisions of which you are aware.

If you are inclined to agree with the borrower's request, note two issues. First, your action should be limited in scope to be as narrow as possible and limited in time to a single instance. Second, it should be made clear that your acquiescence is not to be construed as a part of a course of conduct inconsistent with the loan documents, which may ultimately cause the loan documents to be construed differently than originally intended. If a borrower frequently requests waivers and you frequently agree, it may be appropriate to amend the loan documents because they no longer accurately reflect the intentions of the parties.

Assuming you have reviewed the borrower's specific, written request, have the authority, and wish to accommodate the borrower, consider the following:

a. Respond in writing.
b. Refer specifically to the document and the article or paragraph from which the borrower is seeking relief.
c. Try to avoid the words *waive* or *waiver*, which may not be appropriate.
d. Inform the borrower that, based on its request and on the relevant factors existing at that time, the lender has agreed to (or not to) whatever relief is appropriate.
e. Reserve all of your rights in the future.
f. Make it clear that your letter is (*i*) sent in reference to the specific request in the borrower's letter, (*ii*) sent in reliance on whatever information the borrower delivered in support of its request, (*iii*) limited to this instance only, and (*iv*) not to be implied to be, or construed as, a waiver of or release of any term of any of the loan documents, and except as specifically set forth in your letter, all terms and conditions of the loan documents are ratified and confirmed.

Like notice-letters, waiver-letters are factually intensive and may have very serious legal consequences. It is usually prudent to have the borrower's waiver requests and your written response reviewed by counsel.

FOCUS ON LEGALLY SENSITIVE PROVISIONS

Demand Loans

In theory, a demand obligation may be called by the lender at any time for any reason or for no reason. When, however, language contained in the loan documents appears to be inconsistent with the demand nature of the loan, a court may conclude that the loan is not really a demand loan, and notice may therefore be required. For example, if the note states that it is "due on demand, but if no demand is made, then on (a given future date)" or if the loan agreement contains a list of events of default, or sets forth a default interest rate, or contains affirmative or negative covenants, such language may be deemed inconsistent with the right to demand, and inferences may be raised that negate the demand nature of the instrument. The court may wonder why, if you really wanted the right to demand the obligation at any time, you needed any of these provisions. What did they add?

If you have existing loan documents with this dual personality, to be safe, give notice if you can do so without prejudicing your position. To avoid the issue in the future, consider (1) using a time instrument together with such due dates, events of default, default interest rates and covenants, and like provisions, as you wish, or (2) using a pure demand instrument together with clear and specific language stating that the instrument is due on demand, in all events, and that the other clauses are to be construed cumulatively for the bank's benefit (for example, the covenants assure the continued creditworthiness of the borrower) and not in derogation of its right to demand without notice.

Discretionary Advances

Even where the language of the loan documents makes advances discretionary, the lender may be required, by the rules of good faith and commercial reasonableness, to give the borrower fair notice that future advances will not be made.

In addition, the right to make discretionary advances may be construed in light of other terms in the loan documents. If the loan documents require commitment fees or periodic payments, for example, a court might find these inconsistent with the right to make discretionary advances and infer an obligation on the part of the lender to make the advances.

To avoid this issue, consider committing to make the advances, instead of making them discretionary, but make your agreement subject, in each instance, to the borrower's satisfaction of a list of conditions (ratios, performance covenants, absence of default, etc.) that will give you sufficient comfort.

Acceleration

The right to accelerate the entire indebtedness in the event of default usually causes no problems. The risk lies with the use of language permitting acceleration "at will" or when "insecure." The UCC, in Section

1-208, states that the lender may accelerate at will or when it deems itself insecure *only if it believes in good faith that the prospect of payment or performance is impaired.*

At will If you accelerate pursuant to an "acceleration at will" clause, make sure your file supports your belief, in good faith, that the loan is in jeopardy. This UCC section does not apply to demand instruments; therefore, to avoid the issue, consider casting the instrument as "demand" when appropriate and avoiding the use of the "at will" language. Alternatively, use a time instrument with well-defined events of default tied to performance standards.

Insecurity Like the "acceleration at will" language, an "insecurity" clause is subject to the provisions of UCC Section 1-208, requiring the lender to believe in good faith that the prospect of repayment or performance is impaired. To cover this situation, include in the loan documents a definition of *insecure* or set forth those acts or events that would render the lender insecure (for example, state that a breach of a covenant requiring certain financial ratios to be maintained renders the lender insecure). Your file should then contain information evidencing the breach and supporting your determination of insecurity before the loan is called. Better yet, do not use or rely on the insecurity clause. Whatever would make you feel insecure should be included as an event of default, in the case of a time instrument, or use a demand instrument to which the UCC section does not apply.

Material Adverse Change

This is always a difficult clause on which to rely. It raises lots of questions. What is adverse? What is material? When did it change? Properly drawn documents should answer these questions. To avoid the issue, instead of using the general and broad language of a material adverse change clause, consider not using the clause but, rather, referring to specific performance standards and including them in the form of ratios or affirmative or negative covenants. State that a deviation (as defined) from the required standards on any reporting date is an event of default.

Management Change

When lending to a small corporation, you may have placed substantial weight on the character and abilities of the individuals managing the company and thought it prudent to retain the right to review any future changes in management. If a change in management is included in the loan documents as an event of default, its application should be made very clear. The lender should have the right to declare the default and to accelerate. But then, either do it or do not do it. Do not use the clause as a club to attempt to control existing or replacement management.

PART

III

ENVIRONMENTAL PROBLEMS

Chapter Thirteen

Introduction to CERCLA

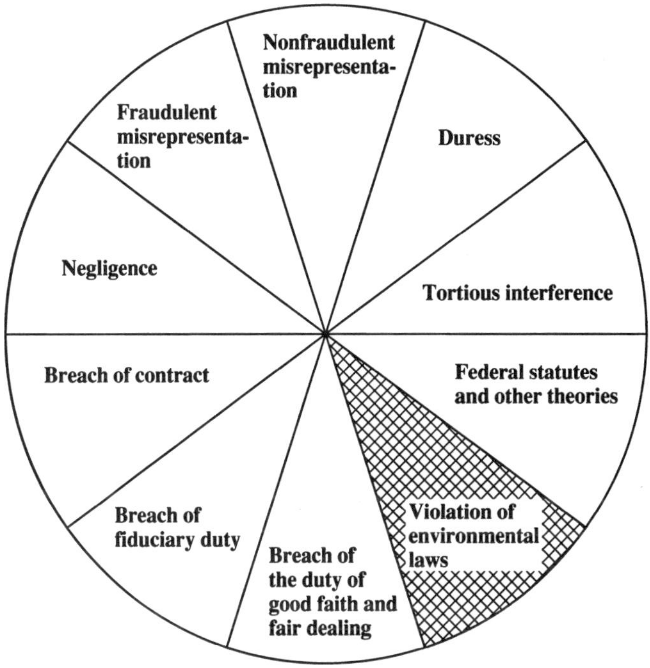

Environmental problems may arise in all kinds of loans. The probability of incurring a problem is increased:

- ***When lending to a borrower engaged in a high-risk activity, such as a garbage collection or chemical business.***
- ***Where the collateral securing the loan is high risk, such as land and buildings that had formerly been used as a paint factory.***

THE BORROWER'S BUSINESS AND YOUR COLLATERAL

Whether it is the business or the collateral that is environmentally sensitive, the lender is at economic risk. When it is the business, consider that large bills received by the borrower for cleanup costs may affect the ability of the borrower to repay the indebtedness. When it is the collateral, the problems are more diverse, and the costs to the lender are potentially enormous.

Traditionally, lenders have looked at the present value of collateral to determine the loan-to-value ratio when evaluating a loan application, and at the future value when determining if they will be made whole in the event of liquidation. Under present law, you must now consider the real possibility that the mere act of taking collateral could expose your institution to cleanup costs far in excess of the amount of the loan or the value of the collateral.

If the proposed collateral *(a)* has an environmental problem, or *(b)* has had an environmental problem in the past, or *(c)* could have a problem in the future, by virtue of its use or intended use or due to its proximity to other environmentally sensitive property, consider all of the following possible effects.

1. The borrower's financial statements listing the collateral as an asset may not be accurate because the market value of the asset may need to be discounted.
2. The borrower's ability to repay the loan may be impaired if its funds are used for cleanup costs.
3. Foreclosure may not be a meaningful option because the collateral may be worth little or nothing.
4. Your institution may not elect to foreclose on the collateral or otherwise involve itself with the business of the borrower because of the risk that *it* will be charged with the cleanup costs.

How, you ask, could the lender possibly become liable for the costs to clean up its collateral? Here's how.

CERCLA

In 1980, Congress enacted the Comprehensive Environmental Response, Compensation, and Liability Act (CERCLA), sometimes referred to as the "Superfund." CERCLA was intended to focus on remedies for cleaning up the environment and the costs of the cleanup. The theory was that if a hazardous waste site was not cleaned by the private sector, the Environmental Protection Agency (EPA) would clean it and then seek reimbursement.

Liability

Liability under CERCLA is *strict*, *joint*, and *several*. These terms collectively mean that one party may be held liable for *all* of the cleanup costs even if it was *not* at fault, or not exclusively at fault, in causing the contamination. If a party is so held liable, it then may attempt to seek contribution from the other responsible parties.

Responsible Parties

CERCLA refers to "responsible parties" as those from whom the EPA may seek reimbursement and specifically includes current and past "owners or operators" of the offending facility. Because owners or operators could include secured lenders that come into title or possession of their collateral, CERCLA provides a specific exclusion to protect lenders that are only involved for the purpose of protecting their collateral. If applicable, this exclusion (known as the "secured lender exemption") has the effect of exempting lenders from the group of responsible parties.

The Secured Lender Exemption Issue

Court decisions have not been consistent, and lenders have been confused as to the meaning of the secured lender exemption. This issue is still not finally resolved.

In 1985, a case (*Mirabile*) construing the secured lender exemption held that so long as the lender did not actively participate in the day-to-day management of the operations of the contaminated facility, it would not be held liable as an owner or operator, even if it participated in the financial affairs of the borrower. Then, in May 1990, a case (*Fleet Factors*) was decided that changed the manner in which the secured lender exemption was to be interpreted; its scope was narrowed, and the risk of lender liability was therefore greater.

A more recent case (*Bergsoe*) addressing the meaning of the exemption was decided in August 1990, and once again lenders seem to have found a new measure of comfort.

A brief review of the development of the applicable case law is helpful in understanding the amorphous state of the law.

The Development of CERCLA Case Law

In *United States* v. *Mirabile*, a 1985 case, a lender foreclosed its mortgage and the real property was transferred to new owners, the Mirabiles. The Mirabiles were notified that drums of toxic waste, left by a previous owner that had used the site as a paint factory, must be removed. After the Mirabiles tried unsuccessfully to clean up, the EPA took over, cleaned the site at a cost of $250,000, and then sued the Mirabiles for reimbursement. The Mirabiles then sued the lender to the paint company that had previously occupied the site.

The thrust of the Mirabiles' claim was that the lender had exercised sufficient financial control to be deemed an owner or operator under CERCLA. The court, examining the activities of the lender, distinguished participation in the general financial matters of the borrower from participation in the management of the facility. Noting that an officer of one lender had visited the site, managed shipments, directed personnel assignments, and recommended manufacturing changes, thus apparently participating in the management of the facility, the court allowed the claim of the Mirabiles to be tried.

Before a final decision on the issue was rendered, the case was settled, but its warning was clear: involvement in the borrower's financial affairs may be acceptable, but participation in the day-to-day management of the facility might subject a lender to liability.

United States v. *Fleet Factors Corp.*, decided in May 1990, involved a factoring arrangement whereby Fleet made a loan to Swainsboro Paint Works. As collateral, Fleet took a security interest in the borrower's real and personal property. After the borrower defaulted and attempted unsuccessfully to reorganize under Chapter 11 of the Bankruptcy Act, the bankruptcy was converted to a Chapter 7 liquidation. Fleet then foreclosed on the inventory and equipment (but not the real property). During the subsequent workout period, the EPA inspected the facility, found toxic chemicals and materials, and spent $400,000 for the cleanup. The EPA then sued Fleet for reimbursement under CERCLA on the grounds that Fleet had become an owner or operator of the facility due to its activities during the workout, even though it was not participating in the day-to-day management of the facility.

The court sided with the EPA and against Fleet, in effect rejecting the *Mirabile* test for liability (participation in the day-to-day management of the facility) and creating a new and broader window of exposure. Now, if the lender had the capacity to control the hazardous substance, it could be held liable for the cleanup costs.

The significance of *Fleet Factors* was twofold. First, as a matter of policy, it demonstrated a feeling by the court that someone was going to reimburse the EPA for the costs of the cleanup of hazardous wastes and that, even if the court had to stretch, lenders were fair game. Second, and more specific, the decision was notice to the lending community that a secured creditor may incur liability without foreclosing on real property. The size of the net used to recover cleanup costs was enlarged (although sewn of a questionable material). The result was that a lender could be liable even if it was not an owner and did not participate in the day-to-day management of the facility, if it had participated in the financial management of the facility to a degree that indicated a capacity to influence the debtor's treatment of hazardous wastes.

Which activities were permissible and which were not was not made clear from the decision. The nature and extent of the allowable lender involvement in the debtor's affairs were not spelled out. The case left lenders without meaningful guidelines other than (1) to have no involvement (and risk losing the value of the collateral) and avoid CERCLA liability or (2) to become involved, attempting to protect the collateral, and risk CERCLA liability.

In re Bergsoe Metal Corporation, decided in August 1990, is kinder to lenders. Bergsoe Metal Corporation ("Bergsoe"), a corporation formed for the purpose of conducting lead recycling operations, arranged for municipal bonds to be issued by The Port of St. Helens (the "Port"), an Oregon municipal corporation empowered to issue industrial revenue bonds to promote industrial development. Through a series of complicated and interlocking loan and security transactions, Bergsoe, the

Port, and United States National Bank of Oregon (the "Bank"), as trustee for the bondholders, completed financing arrangements, as a result of which the Port effectively held title to the land.

Soon after the plant began operating, it experienced financial difficulties, and the Bank put Bergsoe into involuntary bankruptcy under Chapter 11 of the Bankruptcy Act. Thereafter, the Oregon Department of Environmental Quality determined that the plant site had been contaminated by various hazardous substances.

The Bank and the trustee in bankruptcy filed suit against the shareholders of Bergsoe to collect on Bergsoe's debts and to request a declaration that the shareholders were liable for the costs of cleaning up the environmental contamination.

The defendants filed a counterclaim, including a third-party complaint against the Port, alleging that the Bank and the Port were liable for the costs of the cleanup under CERCLA. The Port moved for summary judgment, alleging that it was not an "owner" under CERCLA. The appeal was taken from the district court decision affirming the bankruptcy court's granting of the motion.

The district court first examined the meaning of *owner* under CERCLA and stated that

> The CERCLA definition of "owner" is not . . . coextensive with all uses of that term; it specifically excludes "a person who without participating in the management of . . . a facility, holds indicia of ownership primarily to protect his security in the . . . facility . . . " CERCLA thus protects creditors who do not participate in management of the facility.

The court's analysis held that both parts of a twofold test must be satisfied for the secured lender exemption to apply: (1) the lender must hold the indicia of ownership primarily to protect its security *and* (2) the lender must not have participated in the management of the facility.

As to the first part of the test, the existence of ownership as a security interest, the court acknowledged that while the case involved a somewhat unusual financing arrangement, nevertheless the Port held title for the purpose of securing the payments due by the borrower.

Referring to the second part of the test, the prohibition of participation in management, the court noted that even if the Port held title for the purpose of protecting its security interest, it may still be liable under CERCLA if it participated in management, and "[u]nfortunately, CERCLA does not define the phrase 'participating in the management

. . . of a facility.'" After examining the *Fleet Factors* decision and referring to its ruling as an "intermediate rule" when viewed in light of the extreme positions taken by the parties in that case, the court declined to postulate a new rule, leaving that "for another day." The court did state, however, that "it is clear from the statute that whatever the precise parameters of 'participation,' there must be *some* actual management of the facility before a secured creditor will fall outside the exception."

The fact that the Port had certain rights under its loan documents was held to be irrelevant. What was critical was not what rights the Port had but what it did. Finding no actual acts of management, the court found no liability on the part of the Port.

The decision in *Bergsoe* evidences a dramatic deviation from the holding in *Fleet Factors* and essentially represents a return to the days of the *Mirabile* decision. The problem for lenders, however, has not been solved. While the *Fleet Factors* case and the *Mirabile* case were both federal court decisions, they were rulings in different circuits (*Fleet Factors* in the eleventh and *Bergsoe* in the ninth). Since the U.S. Supreme Court refused to review *Fleet Factors*, we must look for and hope to find a more definitive resolution elsewhere.

Proposed Rules and Pending Legislation

The confusion in the lending community over the issue of potential environmental liability caused certain observable results: *(a)* lenders became more cautious in making loans, some were merely reluctant, and others refused to make environmentally sensitive loans; *(b)* the costs to borrowers increased as lenders demanded environmental audits and other legal assurances; and *(c)* the period between commitment and closing grew longer.

Proposed rules The EPA, in response to the negative impact on the economy caused by lenders making fewer loans, in June 1990 proposed a rule to clarify the application of the secured lender exemption. The draft of the proposed rule would permit lenders to engage in activities to protect their environmentally sensitive collateral, provide credit to borrowers with a known cleanup requirement, and foreclose on defaulted, environmentally sensitive loans, without exposure to liability under CERCLA. If, however, the lender "controlled" or "managed" or "directed" the borrower's environmentally sensitive operation, it could still be liable as an "owner or operator." The proposed EPA rule is a clear rejection of the position taken by the Eleventh Circuit Court of Appeals in *Fleet Factors*. The EPA has been taking comments on the proposed rule, and, as of this writing, the final rule has not been promulgated.

Pending legislation At the same time the EPA was involved in the rule-making process, several bills introduced into the House and Senate were aimed at addressing the lenders' concerns.

On March 14, 1991, Representative John LaFalce (D-NY) introduced H.R. 1450 to amend CERCLA to limit the liability of lending institutions. This bill, which now has over 260 cosponsors, excludes from the definition of *owner or operator* a person who, without participating in the management of a facility, holds indicia of ownership primarily to protect a security interest in such facility. The bill defines *indicia of ownership* as an interest acquired for (1) securing payment of a loan or indebtedness or the performance of an obligation or (2) protecting a security interest.

The proposed EPA rule and the pending legislation are both much needed steps in the direction of clarifying and limiting a lender's potential liability for environmental matters. When—and if—finalized and passed, they should permit lenders to again lend in this hazardous area. Until then, use care in discovering and dealing with environmental matters.

Chapter Fourteen

Discovering and Dealing with Environmental Issues

Think about the possible variations:

- ***You do not know whether an environmental problem exists.***
- ***You are informed that there is no problem (and none surfaces).***
- ***You learn about the existence of the problem prior to making the loan.***
- ***You are informed that there are no environmental problems, make the loan, and then either a preexisting problem is discovered or new contamination occurs.***

It's like being invited to stroll through a mine field! To attempt to survive unscathed, first determine the environmental status of the business and the collateral, and second, determine what to do if there are existing or future problems.

DETERMINING THE ENVIRONMENTAL STATUS

Unlike most lending issues, lenders are not well equipped to determine the existence and extent of environmental problems. While you may be able to analyze balance sheets in your sleep, you probably do not have the technical knowledge or experience required in the area of hazardous wastes. Ordinarily, it is more prudent and a more economical use of your time to request that you be provided with the required information. Do not presume to be an authority in the hazardous area of environmental analysis. Be mindful that environmental matters are high risk and technical, and the legal consequences are in a state of change. You should not, therefore, attempt to shoulder the burden without guidance from your institution, counsel, and environmental experts.

Determining the environmental status of a proposed project or collateral may include

1. Use of an environmental checklist to screen the property.
2. Interviews with the borrower to learn of past, present, or proposed uses or of past or existing environmental problems.
3. Visits to the site to observe any signs of environmental issues involving your borrower's or any neighbor's property.
4. Obtaining an environmental audit (assessment) to learn about any latent contamination, past or pending investigations, and the estimated cost to cure any problems.
5. Obtaining an opinion of borrower's counsel to offer comfort as to the absence of any past or pending problems, and compliance with applicable laws.

TAKING APPROPRIATE ACTION

Once you are on notice of the existence of an environmental risk, then consider *(a)* not making the loan, *(b)* making the loan but minimizing the risk by substituting clean collateral for risky collateral, or *(c)* making the loan after assuring yourself you have obtained appropriate legal and economic protection.

Not making the loan and obtaining pristine collateral are, of course, the safest courses of action. You may elect to make the loan if the risk is relatively small and addressable in a satisfactory manner in the loan documents with a strong likelihood of enforcement and ultimate collection.

Chapter Fifteen

Loan Officer Considerations

The amorphous nature of environmental problems requires that you take advantage of all resources available to avoid problem loans. The suggestions that follow include utilization of the talent and support of your institution, lender's counsel, and environmental consultants.

ASK FOR GUIDANCE FROM YOUR INSTITUTION

Request that your institution adopt and provide you with (and update) an environmental policy. It should provide answers to the following questions: What are environmentally sensitive loans? What types of loans is the lender interested in making? What types of loans will the lender not make? What procedures are to be followed in analyzing different types of businesses and collateral for potential hazardous waste cleanup liability? Which experts are approved to perform environmental studies? What should be requested and received by way of protection for the institution?

TRY TO KEEP CURRENT ON THE STATE OF THE LAW

Request that your institution's counsel periodically provide you with memoranda setting forth explanations of applicable law as it changes. Request that they be clear, simple, precise, and concise. Their purpose should be to guide you in dealing with environmental issues involving your borrower's business or collateral and to inform you when it is time to consult the experts.

VISIT THE SITE

Determine the current use and, to the extent possible, past uses. Look for obvious signs of toxic materials (you probably will not find skulls and crossbones) as well as more subtle signs: vats, drums, leaks, odors, smoke, dead vegetation, soft earth, bubbles on the ground. Look at the neighboring businesses and properties for the same signs.

TALK TO THE BORROWER

Determine what the borrower knows on the subject. Does the borrower now or did it ever use or dispose of hazardous substances? From whom did the borrower buy the property? What business was the seller engaged in? Is the borrower in compliance with all laws? Are there any investigations pending? Has the borrower received any notices from anyone concerning environmental matters?

USE AN ENVIRONMENTAL CHECKLIST

An environmental checklist should set forth the observations and inquiries to be made and the relevant documents to be obtained early in the loan process. It may serve as an early warning that the proposed loan is not one that the lender wishes to make. After completing the checklist, if you still intend to make the loan, a copy of your findings can then be turned over to the professionals conducting the audit or assessment.

USE LEGAL COUNSEL

If you even think your house is on fire, you call the fire department. Feel the same way about calling your institution's counsel. The lawyer or law firm is the expert and will be able to help you. If a problem should arise later, it's nice to have a memo in your file showing that you consulted with counsel and acted on his or her advice.

You cannot and should not be expected to be an expert on all the changes in the law and the meanings of those changes. Counsel can.

MAKE FULL USE OF THE COMMITMENT LETTER

The commitment letter should be used as an investigative tool as well as a substantive legal document. The commitment letter, when signed by the borrower and returned to the lender, may constitute a contract binding the borrower to its terms. You should take advantage of this opportunity to obtain additional information concerning the risks associated with environmental matters and to obtain such comfort as may be possible.

Representations

Include statements in the letter that, when signed, will constitute representations by the borrower to the lender to the effect that (1) the borrower is not and has not been engaged in an environmentally hazardous business, (2) no known hazardous conditions exist or are likely to exist at the borrower's business or property, (3) no notices concerning any environmental matters have been received, (4) to the best of borrower's knowledge, the premises were never used for any environmentally sensitive business or in an environmentally sensitive manner, (5) the borrower has not been threatened by and is not a party to any action or proceeding involving any environmental matters, and (6) the borrower and its property are in compliance with all applicable environmental laws, rules, and regulations and the borrower has all necessary permits or licenses. All of the representations should be made to survive closing.

By including these environmental representations in the commitment letter, you have created another warning device. If a borrower is unable or unwilling to make such representations or if a problem is uncovered at this point in the transaction, you have a head start on its resolution or you can determine not to make the loan. The representations made in the commitment letter should be expanded on and brought to date by the use of a borrower's certificate dated as of the closing date or by including environmental "bring-down" clauses in the loan documents.

Conditions

Use the commitment letter as an escape mechanism. Include language to the effect that it is a condition to the obligation of the lender to make the loan that it be satisfied with the environmental condition of the borrower's business and property. This will allow you to terminate the commitment if environmental problems are discovered or are unmanageable prior to closing.

Opinion of Counsel

The commitment letter should require receipt of (and you should attempt to actually obtain, notwithstanding resistance) an opinion of borrower's counsel, in form and substance satisfactory to the lender, as a condition to lender's obligation to lend. The commitment letter should outline the opinions you wish to receive. Include, among others, that after due investigation and inquiry to the appropriate authorities having jurisdiction, (1) there exist no notices of any environmental issues or problems, (2) no investigations, litigation, or administrative proceedings are threatened or pending against borrower or its property concerning environmental matters, (3) borrower and its property are in compliance with all environmental laws, and borrower has all necessary licenses and permits to operate its business, and (4) counsel has no reason to believe that any environmental problems involving the borrower, its business, or its properties now exist or will arise in the future.

If you obtain a complete and satisfactory environmental audit, you can be more sympathetic to protestations from counsel for the borrower about including environmental matters in the opinion letter.

OBTAIN AN ENVIRONMENTAL AUDIT

When appropriate (or mandated by the lender's guidelines), require an environmental audit (assessment) by a professionally qualified environmental consulting firm. Your visit to the site may only disclose visible or obvious matters, and your discussions with the borrower may disclose little or nothing of value. Be mindful that environmental audits can be expensive relative to the amount of the loan requested. The audit will address latent matters, such as subsurface contamination and problems that require testing to be discerned, such as asbestos, PCBs, or radon. The consultant will search and review building, health, and environmental records on local, state, and federal levels for evidence of problems.

Request that the audit conclude with a meaningful summary, state a conclusion (that the layperson can understand) including the estimated costs to remedy the contamination, and not merely list quantities of toxic substances found. Receipt of an environmental audit, satisfactory in form and substance to the lender, should also be included in the commitment letter as a condition to the lender's obligation to lend.

RETAIN AN ENVIRONMENTAL CONSULTANT

Urge your institution to retain or have available the services of an environmental consultant to review and recommend action in instances where the environmental audit is neither obviously very good nor very bad or where it requires interpretation or evaluation. Neither you nor bank counsel is qualified in environmental engineering or chemical matters.

DO NOT BE THE TRIGGER

While the loan is in good standing, your involvement with the business of the borrower is usually minimal. In the event of default and transfer of the file to workout, the workout officer should be informed that the loan is environmentally sensitive and should be referred to counsel for guidance.

If, however, you are involved with a troubled loan, the law says that you (and your institution) must *not:*

- Participate in the day-to-day management of the facility.
- Control the borrower or involve yourself with the financial management of the facility to the extent a court could conclude that you affected the borrower's use or disposal of hazardous materials.

What does this mean? Keep your distance, remain a professional at all times, consult with counsel. Don't assert control over or involve yourself with the borrower's business by telling the borrower how to run it, making decisions for the borrower, or designating executives or consultants to be employed.

TRY REQUESTING INSURANCE

If your institution is willing to finance high-risk operations, such as hazardous waste disposal sites or chemical plants, consider requiring the borrower to provide appropriate insurance naming the lender as an insured, as a condition to the commitment. Such insurance is not readily available and, if available, is very expensive.

DO NOT RUSH TO FORECLOSE

If you foreclose, you may become an owner or operator and then may be subject to CERCLA liability. The secured lender exemption has been held to be applicable only during the term of the mortgage (when the loan and collateral are still in existence) and not after foreclosure. Since cleanup costs can be substantially more than the indebtedness and more even than the value of the collateral, do not be hasty. Before a decision to foreclose is made on environmentally sensitive property, it may be prudent to obtain or update an environmental audit, including an estimate of cleanup costs.

Chapter Sixteen

Counsel Considerations

The best documents are only as good as their ultimate enforceability and the ability of the borrower or guarantor to pay in accordance with their obligations. Review your loan package for environmentally related issues and suggest that counsel include documents and clauses to provide as much protection as possible.

REPRESENTATIONS AND WARRANTIES

The borrower and all guarantors (as appropriate) should represent and warrant (1) as to the absence of any environmental problems, (2) that borrower and its property are in compliance with all relevant laws and have all necessary permits and licenses, (3) that no notices have been received and that there are no threatened or pending lawsuits or investigations involving the business or property that concern environmental matters, (4) that the site is not used and has not been used (to the best of borrower's or guarantor's knowledge) for any environmentally sensitive use.

INDEMNITIES

The borrower (and all guarantors) should agree to indemnify the lender for all costs related to any aspect of environmental problems. Include costs and expenses incurred in monitoring the borrower's compliance with the loan documents (such as future inspections and audits) and legal expenses incurred related to any environmental matter, including enforcement of any of the lender's rights as well as defending against any actions. The fact that the use of an indemnity clause is no assurance whatsoever of the collection of funds thereunder should not deter you from including it.

COVENANTS

Require covenants by the borrower to the effect that the business shall not use, deal with, or dispose of any hazardous substances and that the site shall not be used (directly or indirectly) for any environmentally hazardous use and that borrower will comply with all environmental laws. Include covenants setting forth the exact obligations of the borrower (and guarantors) to cure any environmental problems that may occur. Require the borrower to give immediate notice in the event any representation or warranty is no longer accurate or in the event the nature of its business changes.

NOTICES

Require that the borrower immediately send the lender copies of any notices received from any governmental authority or private party concerning any environmental matters. This clause is both procedural and substantive. It will give you timely notice of a problem as well as inform you of the nature of the problem, so the lender can enforce its rights under the clauses containing borrower's covenants.

DEFAULT

Include provisions to the effect that any breach by borrower (or any guarantor) of any of the environmental provisions contained in any of the loan documents may be deemed an event of default.

ACCELERATION

Include a provision to the effect that any such default gives the lender the option to accelerate the entire indebtedness. This may enable the lender to be paid before the situation becomes too serious.

NEGATIVE DECLARATION

If the loan transaction involves a sale of real property, consider requiring, as a condition to closing, receipt of a covenant or negative declaration from the seller of the site. The covenant or declaration should state that there have been and are no environmental problems or that they have been addressed and cured. Some states require such a document in connection with certain high-risk transfers. If a document is required by your state, a copy of it and proof of seller's compliance with any applicable laws should be required to be delivered to lender as a condition to closing.

RETAIN RIGHTS TO MONITOR COMPLIANCE

You may wish to assure that in the future the borrower is in compliance with the loan documents and that there remains an absence of environmental problems. Inasmuch as a site inspection only scratches the surface, so to speak, include language to the effect that the borrower not only consents to future inspections, audits, studies, and reports but that it is responsible for the costs of any such future environmental investigations.

SURVIVAL

The foregoing provisions will probably be written to be effective throughout the life of the loan. Consider including language that will assure that the indemnity clauses continue to benefit the lender even after the loan is repaid. Under CERCLA, your institution may continue to be strictly liable as a former owner or operator.

Glossary

acceptance An unequivocal manifestation of willingness to assent to the terms of an offer, given with the intent to be legally bound. In common law contract law, one of the fundamental elements required for the formation of a contract: offer, acceptance, and consideration.

acknowledgment A declaration before an authorized official by the person executing an instrument that it is his or her free act.

actual damages The amount awarded to an injured party for compensation for actual losses. Sometimes referred to as compensatory damages or general damages; may include loss of value, consequential damages, and incidental damages. Distinguish from nominal or punitive (sometimes referred to as exemplary) damages.

agreement An offer that has been accepted.

avoid To be relieved of one's obligations under an agreement. To rescind.

benefit of the bargain A rule of damages (the majority rule) allowing a party to recover loss of profits in an action for fraudulent misrepresentation.

breach The wrongful failure to perform in accordance with the terms of a contract. A breach generally affords the nonbreaching party the right to sue the breaching party.

business coercion A wrongful act or threat that deprives the victim of his or her free will and results in the victim suffering economically. Sometimes referred to as duress or economic duress.

capacity The legal ability to enter into and be bound by the terms of a contract. In contract law, an element required for the formation of a contract. For example, a minor, an insane person, or an intoxicated person may not have contractual capacity.

cause of action The legal theory or grounds on which a lawsuit is based.

CERCLA The Comprehensive Environmental Response, Compensation, and Liability Act, adopted by Congress in 1980.

common law Law composed of decisions of courts based on customs and usages from time immemorial. Distinguish from law derived from legislative bodies (statutes).

compensatory damages Damages calculated to compensate an injured party for his or her injury. Sometimes referred to as actual damages; may include loss of value, consequential damages, and incidental damages. Distinguish from nominal and punitive (sometimes referred to as exemplary) damages.

condition A future and uncertain event upon the happening of which is made to depend the existence or extinguishment of a legal obligation.

consequential damages Damages that do not flow directly from the wrongful act of the defendant, but from the consequences of that act; for example, lost profits. Distinguish from incidental damages, which flow directly from the defendant's wrongful act.

consideration The promise or act that induces another to enter into a contract; assuming a new legal duty or relinquishing an existing legal right. In common law contract law, one of the fundamental elements required for the formation of a contract: offer, acceptance, and consideration.

contract An agreement that the law will enforce. The fundamental elements are, at common law, offer, acceptance, and consideration.

counterclaim A claim made by a defendant to oppose or reduce the claim of the plaintiff.

covenant An agreement, usually in writing, that something is or shall be done.

damage The loss or injury to a person or property caused by another. Distinguish from damages.

damages The monetary remedy sought by the plaintiff in a lawsuit. Distinguish from damage.

deceit The false representation of a material fact, made with knowledge of its falsity and an intent to deceive, that is justifiably relied on by and causes damage to another. Sometimes referred to as fraud or fraudulent misrepresentation.

default The failure to comply with a legal requirement.

defendant The party against whom a lawsuit is brought. The party bringing the lawsuit is the plaintiff.

duress An improper threat or act that coerces a person to act against his or her will. Sometimes called economic duress or business coercion.

duty An obligation owed to another.

duty of good faith and fair dealing A theory of lender liability derived from three sources: contract law, tort law, and the Uniform Commercial Code. All contracts, by implication, impose on the parties the duty of good faith and fair dealing.

economic duress A wrongful act or threat that deprives the victim of his or her free will and results in the victim suffering economically. Sometimes referred to as duress or business coercion.

exemplary damages Damages that may be imposed against a party as a punishment or to set an example. Sometimes referred to as punitive damages.

express Manifested by words, either written or oral, as in an express contract. Distinguish from implied.

fact A past event, definitely ascertainable and verifiable.

fiduciary A person or institution in a position of trust; one who must exercise a fiduciary duty.

fiduciary duty A duty of utmost care and good faith, required of fiduciaries.

fraud in the inducement The false misrepresentation of a material fact, made with knowledge of its falsity and an intent to deceive, that is justifiably relied on by and causes damage to another. Sometimes referred to as fraud, fraudulent misrepresentation, or deceit.

fraudulent misrepresentation The false representation of a material fact, made with knowledge of its falsity and an intent to deceive, that is justifiably relied on by and causes damage to another. Sometimes referred to as fraud, fraud in the inducement, or deceit.

good faith Honesty in fact. Conduct that does not violate community standards of reasonableness, fairness, or decency.

implied Manifested by conduct, as in implied contract. Distinguish from express.

incidental damages Damages that flow directly from the wrongful act of the defendant. Distinguish from consequential damages, which do not flow directly from the defendant's wrongful act.

indemnity To reimburse a person for a loss incurred.

legality of purpose An element required for the enforceability of an agreement. For example, an agreement made for a criminal, tortious, or other purpose contrary to public policy is not enforceable.

lender liability A recognized area of the law by which a lender may be held liable for its wrongful acts.

loss of profits An element of consequential damages.

loss of value An element of compensatory damages. The difference between the value of the promised performance and the value of the actual performance received.

negligence Conduct that falls below the standard established by the law for protection against an unreasonable risk of harm. The elements of negligence are duty of care, breach of that duty, damage, and a causal relationship between the breach of duty and the damage.

nonfraudulent misrepresentation The false representation of a material fact, carelessly made, that is justifiably relied on by and causes damage to another. Sometimes referred to as negligent or innocent misrepresentation.

notary public A public officer empowered to certify and administer oaths and to take acknowledgments.

offer The communication of a promise, the terms of which are definite and certain, together with that which is expected in return, given with the intent to be legally bound. In common law contract law, one of the fundamental elements required for the formation of a contract: offer, acceptance, and consideration.

out-of-pocket damages Damages calculated as the difference between the value received and the value given; does not include loss of profit.

plaintiff The party who brings a lawsuit. The party against whom the lawsuit is brought is the defendant.

prima facie (Latin) A state of facts presumed to be true unless disproved by evidence to the contrary.

promise An unequivocal statement that something will or will not occur in the future.

punitive damages Damages that may be awarded against a party as punishment or to set an example. Sometimes referred to as exemplary damages.

representations and warranties Statements of fact that induce another to enter into a contract.

rescind To be relieved of one's obligations under an agreement. To avoid.

scienter (Latin) Knowingly. One of the elements of fraudulent misrepresentation; the misrepresentation must be made with knowledge of its falsity and an intent to deceive.

tort A private or civil wrong against a person or property. Distinguish from a crime, which is a violation of public law.

tortious Describes a wrong that is private or civil; as in tortious interference.

tortious interference (with contract) The intentional and improper interference with the performance of a contract or prospective contractual relationship causing a person not to perform the contract or to enter into the relationship.

Uniform Commercial Code A uniform law drafted by the National Conference of Commissioners on Uniform State Laws governing commercial transactions. Sometimes referred to as the UCC.

waiver The voluntary and intentional relinquishment of a right.

Index